HISTORY IS MY WITNESS

# History is my Witness

Foreword by
James Cameron

Edited by
Gordon Menzies

British Broadcasting Corporation

This book has been published in conjunction with
a series on BBC 1 (Scotland) 'History is my Witness'.

First broadcast on Thursdays from 6 January to 3 February 1977.
The series is produced by Gordon Menzies.

Published to accompany a series of programmes prepared in consultation
with the BBC Broadcasting Council for Scotland

Published by the
British Broadcasting Corporation
35 Marylebone High Street
London W1M 4AA

ISBN 0 563 16077 2

First published 1976
© The authors 1976

Printed in England by
Western Printing Services Ltd, Bristol

This book is set in 11 on 12 point Monotype Garamond

# Contents

*James Cameron*

# FOREWORD

In spite of all the legends and the humbug, in spite of the romance and the sentiment and the histrionics and the comic singers and the black despair, all equally disguised in jest and tears, Scotland is above all a country of irony. It can be bitterly cruel. It can be compassionate, when it suits its purpose. Its paradox is to be at the same time impossibly arrogant and unreasonably coy. Scotland has spent many years trivialising itself, in a wholly unnecessary effort to establish an image acceptable to outsiders, when it should be proclaiming the dignity of its institutions, and particularly the law.

Everyone knows that Scottish law differs from that of England, and in some very significant ways, but sometimes one forgets how different it is, and was, how varied was the mood in which it was applied in the past, with what a particular passion social change was resisted here, and promoted there. Somehow the strange sonorous language of the old Scottish Courts uniquely project the poetry of the pedantic. The tale of Scottish jurisprudence is one of the meaningful aspects of this sardonic nation's history.

This book tells the story of five major causes that led to five memorable trials. Or rather, four trials and an Official Enquiry that, as it turned out, amounted to a trial. Each one says something different about the nature of Scottish society at the time, and of the Scottish character, and of the Scottish conflicts; sometimes of Scottish hypocrisy.

In a sense it reinforces the idea that Scotland has had a strange tenacity to lost causes. This is only partly true. Two only of these important cases involve formal politics, and of them one only remotely. Nevertheless it is part of Scots mythology that everything in the past should be somehow identified with rue and regret. Even the collapse of the Tay Bridge ended in useless recrimination; even the trial of Madeleine Smith ended in an historic uncertainty. They were in their way the most memorable of these great debates, yet they were at the same time the most trivial.

Of the *dramatis personae* involved in these collected cases, which span almost exactly a century, the most apparently attractive – indeed the only one with any claim to charm – is Thomas Muir, the earnest young leader of the

Movement for Parliamentary Reform. In the latter days of the eighteenth century under the Pitt administration this was indeed a clamant need. Scotland was only just becoming aware of how rotten its politics were, how corrupt and unrepresentative were the Burghs. It was a fruitful time for protest: two potent examples had just been resoundingly successful, the French and the American Revolutions. Tom Paine in his *Rights of Man* had declared that Governments *could* be changed under pressure.

It was a propitious moment for the appearance of Thomas Muir, the young Glasgow lawyer, to turn up in the Society of the Friends of the People – needless to say, greatly concerning the Establishment, which was already uneasy at the precedent of the French Revolution. Thomas Muir was promptly put under the surveillance of the eighteenth-century equivalent of the Special Branch. He was arrested in 1793 for sedition, bailed, whereupon he went to Paris with, apparently, the extraordinary perverse notion of saving Louis XVI. Paris seems so to have gone to his head that he was even late for his own trial. There is something characteristically and even sublimely dotty about the whole situation.

The Edinburgh trial was, to be sure, a travesty, a simple eighteenth-century version of the contemporary Show Trial. The Judge was partisan, the jury was packed, the prosecution overtly political. Thomas Muir conducted his own defence as a campaign. He was sentenced to transportation for fourteen years.

Muir was probably no great political theorist, no great polemicist; he was not without flaws; but he introduced his dreams of Parliamentary reform to the working people of Scotland, and proclaimed them bravely. Of the characters in this book of small dramas he alone was a positive.

Thomas Muir escaped from his exile in Australia to America, thence to France, where he died almost forgotten at thirty-three. It seems a short life to have included so much.

Patrick Sellar was a total contrast. The trial of Patrick Sellar was not so much the trial of a man as of a social calamity. The 'Clearances' of the Western Highlands of Scotland have receded into the past just long enough to be conveniently forgotten – except of course by those Highlanders who can still muster up an ancestral memory of the last accepted act of genocide within the United Kingdom. As Ian Grimble says in his account of the Sellar trial, legend and fact have become inextricably interwoven. Even though Patrick Sellar died as recently as 1851, his name has gone into the Gaelic folklore of imprecation. He destroyed people, they say, to make room for sheep. He was curiously unimportant, except as a symbol of a barbarous system.

After Culloden, Scotland was demoralised; after the excesses of the Butcher Cumberland the nation was in a state of shock. John Prebble, who wrote far and away the best book on both periods, said: 'Once the chiefs had lost their powers many of them lost also any personal interest in their clansmen. During the next hundred years they continued the work of Cumberland's battalions. So that they might lease their glens and braes to sheep farmers from the Lowlands and England, they cleared the crofts of men, women and children, using police and soldiers where necessary.'

Patrick Sellar was merely an instrument of this process. He was Factor to the infamous Countess of Sutherland, landlord of that huge but remote region that had prudently taken little part in the Jacobite romanticism. The Highlanders of Sutherland were cruelly used and betrayed; they were 'no longer to be considered as of any advantage over sheep or other useful animal'.

In clearing his lands of people Patrick Sellar's methods seem to have gone over the top even by the standards of the day. To Sellar, a Lowlander who did not even speak the crofters' language, they were aboriginals to be evicted or destroyed or burned out or intimidated into flight. He would seem to have been a kind of Rachman of his age. However, in the end he went too far and was obliged to stand trial for culpable homicide. He was, almost inevitably, acquitted, with what amount to a congratulation from the Bench. The deserts from which the Sutherland peasants were driven are there to see to this day, lovely and, of course, still empty.

There is no point in cataloguing these stories; each one has its own atmospheric message. The tale of the Glasgow Spinners synthesises as well as can be the ferocious industrial conditions of the 1830s, where a spinner might start work at eight or nine years old, never make more than forty shillings a week, and rarely live over forty. To attempt to form a trade union was an unlawful act of 'combination or conspiracy'.

Dreadful though the work was, those who did it went to great lengths to keep it to themselves, and sinister 'protection' rackets developed. Occasionally, as in the case of this incident and subsequent trial, someone got killed. And here again the trial of the Glasgow Spinners for 'illegal conspiracy, intimidation, threats, and murder' is not so much the trial of individuals as of a system.

The one episode in this collection with which I can claim a sort of remote association is that of the great Tay Bridge disaster of 1879, since I lived for some years hard by Magdalen Green in Dundee, the northern landfall of the Bridge, and as a young man on the local paper it fell to my lot to re-tell the old Disaster story on its every anniversary, which seemed to me *ad infinitum*. To this day I can recount it almost from memory.

The Tay Bridge itself was an intrinsic part of the commercial battle between the North British and Caledonian Railways. For travellers on the old N.B. the northward journey entailed two tiresome and time-consuming river ferries. The Caledonian customers went direct by way of Perth. The Tay Bridge was intended to be the answer: the longest and greatest bridge in the world, the supreme Victorian industrial triumph. Two miles across, six years to build. And within a year of its completion it had fallen into the Firth of Tay, carrying with it the 5.20 p.m. from Burntisland to Dundee: an engine, five carriages, a brake-van, and seventy-five people.

The Board of Trade enquiry took twenty-five days to reveal an appalling story of mismanagement, dishonesty, sloppy workmanship and contractual fiddles. It is true that the terrible storm of that Sunday, 28 December 1879, would have imposed a ferocious strain on the best of engineering, and this was clearly not the best. The inevitable scapegoat was the bridge's designer, Thomas Bouch. In its report to Parliament the Court of Enquiry did not spare him.

'This bridge was badly designed, badly constructed, and badly maintained, and its downfall was due to its inherent defects . . . for all these defects Sir Thomas Bouch is mainly to blame. . . .'

Four months later Sir Thomas Bouch, too, was dead, bringing the total number of victims claimed by the bridge in its making and in its construction to ninety-six in all.

With the famous Trial of Madeleine Smith we are once again on pretty familiar ground, since it has long been among the classics for connoisseurs of these affairs. And here again, too, what is held up for examination is less the guilt or innocence of one demure and well-to-do young woman but the splendidly typical responses of a Victorian Scottish bourgeois society which was, in effect, not trying Madeleine Smith for murdering her lover but for having one.

The trial, of course, also became celebrated as the textbook example of that peculiar quiddity of Scottish criminal law: the Third Verdict, which means that the accused is neither Innocent nor Guilty, but the case is Not Proven. The jury, in a word, concludes: we know she did it, but they didn't establish it, and in any case the laddie maybe deserved it. Technically it leaves the prosecution open to have another go later, but they never did.

The trial of Madeleine Smith proved nothing, except that a pretty and self-possessed woman could take on the big battalions of middle-class morality, and if she did not defeat them, she held them to a good draw.

JAMES CAMERON

## EDITOR'S NOTE

This book arose out of a television series of the same name, produced by BBC Scotland's educational broadcasting department. It is also introduced by James Cameron in his own inimitable style. The television series relies extensively on reconstructed courtroom drama of the actual proceedings, on counsel's speeches, on the examination and cross-examination of witnesses, on verdicts by judges and juries. The articles in this book fill in the background to the trials and at the same time provide a fascinating insight into social, political and industrial conditions in nineteenth-century Scotland. Although each writer has made a special study of his subject the issues are all highly controversial, involving as they do politics, agricultural 'improvements', trade unionism, murder, morality and the reputation of Victorian engineering.

I have conceived my task as editor as one of encouraging the authors to keep the general reader in mind without lowering their own academic standards and of streamlining the resulting contributions. I have been greatly assisted by their co-operation and forbearance. Many people in and outwith the BBC itself have also contributed to the production of this book and to all concerned I am truly grateful.

The four trials and the Board of Trade inquiry into the Tay Bridge Disaster have to be seen and understood in the context of their time. The abiding fascination of the law is that it is primarily concerned with people and no doubt the arguments will continue over the motivation and judicial treatment of the personalities involved in these trials. History might indeed be their witness but the verdicts remain enshrined forever.

GORDON MENZIES

# Thomas Muir

## Ken Logue

On 26 January 1799 the Mayor of Chantilly entered a death in the town register.

At six o'clock in the morning a stranger died in this commune, that they only know from hearsay that he was called Thomas Muir, that none of them knows his place of birth, his country or his age. . . .

Thomas Muir had drifted into poverty and obscurity in the little town of Chantilly, 25 miles north of Paris. He was only thirty-three. He had been found at six o'clock that morning by a boy of twelve. The boy reported it to the postman who knew from letters and newspapers he delivered that his name was Thomas Muir. No one in Chantilly knew any more.

Thomas Muir is remembered for the prominent part he played in the early parliamentary reform movement and for his role as a 'political martyr' at the hands of the Pitt administration in Scotland. While at Glasgow University he gained political experience and learned something about the possibility of political change. As the leader of the students who championed the cause of one of the popular professors, John Anderson, against the rest of the faculty, he acquired practical experience as a speaker and as a leader. From another professor, John Millar, he learned that political change was possible and might become necessary. Millar was a man who sympathised with the lot of ordinary people. He expressed that sympathy by defending strikers in the courts, by encouraging reading societies and, later, by anonymous political pamphleteering. Much of that sympathy rubbed off on Muir. The young student leader had intended to become a minister but when he was expelled from Glasgow for his political activities this became impossible. He turned instead to the bar and after studying law in Edinburgh, was admitted in 1787 as a member of the Faculty of Advocates. Between that date and 1792, when he became actively involved in the reform movement, he practised as a fluent and eloquent but unremarkable advocate.

These five years saw the first stirrings of political awareness in Scotland. The American War of Independence, the Burgh Reform Movement and the

French Revolution all played their part in this process. That the political state of Scotland was bad in the late eighteenth century is illustrated by a contemporary review of each of the Scottish constituencies. This revealed that the thirty county Members of Parliament in Scotland were elected by only 2,662 voters while the remaining fifteen burgh representatives were chosen by the self-appointing and corrupt town-councils of the royal burghs. In this sort of situation it is not surprising that one man should manage to engross political power. That man was Henry Dundas, friend and ally of William Pitt. He had been at various times in his career Lord Advocate in Scotland, Home Secretary, Secretary for India and the Secretary for War and the Colonies. Judging everything in terms of power and expediency he began in the 1770s using patronage and connections to build up his electoral support in Scotland. In the 1780s he extended his influence even further. He used a detailed knowledge of Indian affairs to extend the patronage at his disposal and this in turn made him an indispensable ally of Pitt. In 1784 Dundas could bring Pitt twenty-two out of forty-five Scottish seats for his interest while by 1790 he could contribute thirty-four.

It is to the American War of Independence that the first signs of general political awakening in Scotland can be traced. The war had two effects. At first it was generally supported but as time went on and there were no signs of a successful conclusion, opinion began to alter. The failure of the administration to crush the rebels began to be seen as evidence of the mismanagement of affairs by an unresponsive and unrepresentative government. At the same time attention was drawn to the democratic ideals for which the colonists were fighting. In Scotland a movement began in the 1780s to reform the corrupt and totally unrepresentative nature of the local government of the Scottish burghs. Its first aim was to extend the power of electing the burgh M.P.s not to the whole male population but to the burgesses or substantial members of the burgh community. The movement went on to demand the internal reform of the self-perpetuating town-councils whose conduct of local affairs was at least irresponsible and often illegal. A Bill to reform the Scottish burghs was introduced into the House of Commons by the playwright Sheridan but it was easily stifled there by Henry Dundas.

The burgh reformers had specifically excluded any ideas of universal suffrage. It was not until revolution broke out in France that the ordinary people of Scotland and the rest of Britain began to show an active and widespread interest in political reform. The events in France were followed assiduously in the newspapers. In 1789 most sections of the community welcomed the French Revolution which many believed was similar in nature to Britain's so-called Glorious Revolution in 1688 and few saw as a serious threat to the *status quo*. It was only slowly that the propertied classes in Britain began to realise the potential threat posed by the new political order which emerged in France. No such doubts assailed the bulk of the poorer sections of society for whom the French Revolution was a revelation. There existed in Scotland a deep-rooted egalitarianism and, with the example of France before them, many Scots saw that this could be translated into political democracy.

In his *Reflections on the Revolution in France*, Edmund Burke was the first to warn the established and propertied part of society of the dangers inherent in the French Revolution. This work appeared in November 1790 and three months later a famous radical reply was published – the first part of Tom Paine's *Rights of Man*. This book, which was completed a year later with part two, was to influence thousands of ordinary working people as well as activists in the struggle for parliamentary reform which was just then beginning. Paine's *Rights of Man* attacked Burke's reactionary view of the French Revolution and set out in fresh and vigorous style its democratic ideals so that everyone could understand them. He dismissed the British constitution as nothing more than a fraud since it made a mockery of representation. He argued that the ruling political oligarchy could not be expected to reform itself and that the only real solution was a general convention elected by all the people to consider the government of the country and to reform it. As well as the intoxicating political message, Paine's work had a social vision which included family allowances, free education for everyone and old-age pensions. By 1793 sales of the *Rights of Man* had reached 200,000 throughout Britain, the circulation being stimulated rather than stifled by a Royal Proclamation against it in May 1792. In Scotland the egalitarian assumptions implicit in Paine's book made it particularly sought after and extracts were published as broadsheets which probably passed through many different hands. It is thought to have appeared in a rough Gaelic translation. For many people Paine put into words inchoate thoughts about the French Revolution, for others he opened their eyes to the nature of society but for all ordinary people he pointed to the possibility of far-reaching changes.

1792 was the year in which the movement for parliamentary reform became, finally, a popular movement in which the ordinary people of Britain took an active part. This manifested itself in Scotland in two major ways: firstly by the establishment of societies of Friends of the People and secondly by the often violent expression of democratic sentiment in disturbances and demonstrations. The Tree of Liberty, the French symbol of liberty, equality and fraternity, was planted in towns and villages all over Scotland. In other demonstrations in support of democratic reform effigies of government ministers, particularly of Henry Dundas, were burnt. In May 1792 Lanark was in a state of turmoil and disorder for nearly eight days because of 'an almost universal Spirit of Reform'. Over and over again, at Aberdeen, Perth, Dundee and many other places in the northern part of the country, Dundas was burned in effigy. The most serious outbreak of popular hostility to the established government and support for the ideas of the French Revolution took place in Edinburgh over the period 4, 5 and 6 June 1792. Preceded by a flood of anonymous handbills and letters urging people to demonstrate in favour of democracy, there were three days of sporadic rioting during which Dundas was again burned in effigy and the houses of both the Lord Advocate and the Lord Provost were attacked by large crowds. These and other disturbances indicate a groundswell of popular opinion in favour of reform. It was against this background that Thomas Muir and his friends began to organise societies to agitate for parliamentary reform.

On 3 October 1792 Thomas Muir was elected vice-president of the newly formed Glasgow Society of Friends of the Constitution and of the People. Earlier, in July, he had been active in setting up a similar society in Edinburgh. The societies of Friends of the People in Scotland, although the same in name as the London Society of Friends of the People, were established on very different lines. The London society was a select body of M.P.s, country gentlemen and professional men paying 2 guineas a year in subscriptions and aiming to offset what they saw as the unconstitutional extremism of Paine. The Scottish societies were based much more closely on the older and much more popular London Corresponding Society. The societies of Friends of the People in Scotland were popular and democratic, because subscriptions were kept very low and there were no social barriers to membership. In reporting the setting up of the Glasgow Society, a government supporter gave expression to the fear which was to be the downfall of both the Friends of the People and of Thomas Muir and other leading reformers. Writing to Edinburgh he commented that—

the success of the French Democrats has had a most mischievous Effect here . . . it has led them to think of founding societies into which the lower Class of People are invited to enter – and however insignificant these leaders may be in themselves, when backed with the Mob they become formidable.

The government did not fear a few political 'renegades' like Thomas Muir or the Glasgow Society's president, Lieutenant-Colonel Dalrymple of Fordell. It was, however, almost panic-stricken by the thought that, with such leadership, the ordinary people of Britain might emulate their French counterparts. Events in France were showing that, no matter how innocuous initial moves towards reform might be, the people soon demanded more radical changes.

Thomas Muir, having once publicly entered reform politics, had no intention of giving up. At the beginning of November 1792 he confirmed the worst fears of government by encouraging the setting up of societies of

Friends of the People in the area around his home at Huntershill, near Glasgow. On 3 November he addressed the newly formed Kirkintilloch society. At around the same time he visited the societies in Campsie and Paisley. What he actually said at these meetings, attended by and large by young hand-loom weavers, was of course one of the subjects of his later trial. Most witnesses, both prosecution and defence, agree that Muir's speeches were perfectly proper in the sense that he did not urge his listeners to any unlawful acts. He criticised the blatantly unrepresentative nature of the parliamentary franchise in Britain in general and in Scotland in particular. He compared the British with the French constitution and concluded, a little optimistically, that more equal representation in France meant less taxation. He explained to the meetings that the sole aim of the societies of the Friends of the People was to win more equal representation in shorter parliaments and that the way to achieve this was by petitioning Parliament and by publicising their views as widely as possible. He usually concluded by recommending order and regularity among reformers both in meetings of the society and outside. It would be, he argued, counterproductive for the Friends of the People to

*Huntershill House (Muir's home)*

indulge in or condone riot, disturbance or direct action. Whether this sort of warning was sincere or simply said to cover himself in the future, we shall never know, but there are several things which tend to indicate his sincerity. In the first place there is no record of his having said anything which might be construed as incitement: he may have said things which disturbed and upset the government but that is not the same as fomenting disturbances. Furthermore, the most important influence on Muir's thought was probably Professor John Millar, the 'apostle of liberalism', who was a bourgeois reformer rather than a violent revolutionary. Finally Muir himself was a middle-class professional lawyer whose aim was the reform of parliamentary representation and he showed some contempt for those who extended 'political equality' to mean 'an equal distribution of property'.

Muir spent most of the period from October 1792 until his arrest in January 1793 in Edinburgh, where he seems to have expended a lot of time and energy attending various meetings of societies of Friends of the People. At one meeting in Blackfriars Wynd a government spy, reporting on the speeches given, commented that 'Mr Muir's in particular was a long one', but moderate in tone. On 22 November a meeting of delegates from the societies in and around Edinburgh was held in Lawrie's Dancing School, James Court. Various speeches were made, again including one from Muir. The government spy himself reported that—

These speeches were chiefly directed to admonishing the People with respect to their behaviour in the present critical situation of affairs and strongly enjoining temperance and moderation – intimating that if any who had joined should be concerned in promoting or being in any Riot that they would be expelled.

The reformers in general were very concerned that they should be seen to be acting responsibly and constitutionally. The belief was that by such behaviour and the presentation of a sober and respectful petition they would achieve their purpose. A secondary argument was that if this approach failed then there would be a surge of support in the country which the government would not be able to resist further. If others merely thought that the time was not yet ripe for action they did not share their views with government spies or air them in public places.

The most important decision taken at the James Court meeting was to call a general or Scottish Convention of delegates from all over Scotland to consider an address to Parliament. As a result the first full Scottish Convention of Societies of Friends of the People met in Lawrie's Dancing School on 11, 12 and 13 December 1792. Over 150 delegates attended from nearly 70 different societies. Because of the expense of sending delegates, the Convention was dominated by members from Glasgow and Edinburgh but there were delegates from all over central Scotland. Thomas Muir was named as a delegate from both Dundee and from the Canongate No. 1 society. One of the first things the Convention decided was to rotate the chairmanship from meeting to meeting, in line with their principles of liberty and political equality. Colonel Dalrymple was elected the chairman for the first day.

As far as Muir was concerned the most important item of business came on the second day of the Convention when he presented the *Address from the Society of United Irishmen to the Delegates for Promoting a Reform in Scotland*. At this time the United Irishmen formed a society not dissimilar to the Friends of the People and its aim was to throw open the Irish Parliament to all Irishmen irrespective of rank and religion. The movement later became a revolutionary one but in December 1792 it was still trying to act within the constitution. When Muir proposed reading the *Address* to the Convention Colonel Dalrymple and others objected as they thought it contained treason or at least 'misprision of treason' (concealing knowledge of treason). Muir, in countering this, said that he took upon himself the whole responsibility and the whole danger of the measure. Although this assumption of responsibility was probably worthless, the Convention minutes tell us that 'the cry to hear it was universal'. And so the *Address* was read.

It began by paying tribute to the Scottish reform movement and honoured those who were struggling in the cause of liberty in Scotland. 'Our cause is your cause' it said, comparing the totally inadequate parliamentary representation of both Scotland and Ireland. It recounted the changing nature of British supremacy in Ireland, first through military force and then by systematic corruption, and explained how Catholic and Protestant were now united to seek justice for Catholics and reform of parliament for all. 'British supremacy takes alarm' – and is trying to divide and rule by appealing to the idea of the Protestant Ascendancy. The United Irishmen, however, remain united in the cause of liberty and equal representation. They suggest that in each country, Scotland, England and Ireland, the people should meet in Constitutional Conventions, send delegates to discuss a plan of reform and then present this as a unanimous petition to Parliament. The *Address* concluded with a request that the Scottish Convention reply to their suggestions as soon as possible.

When Muir had finished several people commented that it may, indeed, have contained treason and hoped that the Convention would have nothing more to do with it. One exchange between Robert Fowler, an Edinburgh delegate, and Muir is interesting for the light it throws on the attitudes of Muir and of the more moderate Friends of the People. Fowler quoted from the *Address*, referring to Scotland's waking interest in reform.

not by a *calm*, contented, secret wish for a reform in parliament, but by openly, actively, and urgently *willing* it, with the unity and energy of an *embodied* nation.

The words, he insisted, could be construed as high treason. Muir's response was firstly that Scotland was an 'embodied nation' since it had its own legal system. Secondly he argued that M.P.s will a reform, the Friends of the People will a reform, the people of Scotland and Ireland will a reform and they petition parliament to translate the will into a reality – 'Is it treason to petition Parliament?' he concluded. These arguments are, to say the least, simplistic. Muir appeared to be assuming that there were self-evident truths contained in the British constitution. The existence of the whole reform movement belied that assessment. As events were to show it is the ruling establishment which decides whether petitioning parliament is or is not treason, or perhaps just sedition. Fowler was clearly a cautious man but his assessment of the situation of the reformers was more realistic than that of Thomas Muir. Having heard the debate about the *Address*, the Convention decided that it was in places too extreme. They therefore asked Muir to return it to the United Irishmen, pointing out the passages which the Convention could not accept in their present form.

As far as the Convention was concerned that was the end of the matter and it went on to discuss at some length a set of resolutions drawn up by a specially appointed committee. During the debate Muir placed himself firmly in the camp of those reformers who subscribed to the 'Norman yoke' theory of constitutional history. That is he believed that the British constitution was basically a good one which had originated in the days of Anglo-Saxon freedom. This free constitution had been undermined by the Norman Conquest and subsequent authoritarian regimes. Although this was basically an English constitutional doctrine, Muir argued that Scotland too had had a free constitution and that in these halcyon days a Scots free man was more free than an English free man. Another aspect of Muir which was revealed during the Convention was his slight impatience with its democratic basis. In spite of his expressed view that the Convention should not place its trust in any one person or group, Muir was instrumental in establishing such a group. He and a few others proposed the setting up of a permanent committee structure to continue the work of the Convention between sittings. Committees of finance were thus set up, giving considerable powers to a relatively small body of people among whom Thomas Muir was likely to be prominent. It can be argued that Muir and his friends were displaying a desire to influence the course of the reform movement beyond that which they could exert in the full Convention.

On the last day of the Convention, an interesting and important incident took place. The resolutions of the Goldsmith Hall Association were brought to the attention of the Convention. The Goldsmith Hall Association was a group of loyalists and anti-reformers that had been very actively encouraged by the Government. The resolutions called for the support of all who supported the 'happy constitution', who opposed the dissemination of 'false and delusive opinions' and who wished to counteract sedition, riot and tumult. The Convention decided that there was nothing in the resolutions with which they disagreed and therefore several members were sent out to subscribe to them. Each of the delegates who signed, including Thomas Muir, did so with 'delegate of the Society of the Friends of the People' after his name. The Goldsmith Hall Association later refused any signatures with that addition and deleted those that had already been made. In the course of the last evening of the Convention anxious requests were made by some county delegates for a definite commitment by the Convention to petition Parliament. It was decided, however, to await the outcome of the petition of the London Society of the Friends of the People before taking any action in Scotland. After the Convention agreed to publish its resolutions and minutes, the meeting closed on a highly emotional note. The whole Convention rose and holding up their hands took an oath 'to live free or die!' The Convention adjourned until the following April.

After the Convention Thomas Muir was a marked man. A few days after it closed Robert Dundas, the Lord Advocate, wrote to Henry Dundas, the Home Secretary. As soon as he could get a copy of the Irish Address, 'Mr Solicitor (General) and I are resolved to lay Muir by the heels on a Charge of High Treason'. A few days later the Sheriff of Edinburgh reported that a letter meant for Thomas Muir of Huntershill had been delivered to Muir of Warriston. It had been opened and sent on. At first it was supposed to have been a letter from Forfar acknowledging receipt of pamphlets and assuring Muir that 2,000 men were ready at his command. Less dramatically but equally damning for Thomas Muir in the eyes of authority it transpired that the letter was from Kirkintilloch, acknowledging receipt of pamphlets and reporting that membership of the Friends of the People was now 50 'steady patriots'. Information on Muir's activities was eagerly sought by the Government. The story reached Edinburgh that Muir had set up his own blacksmith's shop and public house in order to display reform propaganda. He had asked a smith and farrier, who kept a public house on the Glasgow–Edinburgh road, to post up copies of the Declaration of the Rights of Man. When he had refused, Muir had set up in opposition across the road.

Investigations were made in and around Glasgow about Muir's activities, particularly with reference to the intercepted Kirkintilloch letter. Then on 2 January 1793, Muir was arrested. He refused to answer any questions, declared his commitment to parliamentary reform and was released on bail. In the days after his arrest Thomas Muir attended several dispirited meetings of the Friends of the People. The Government's two-pronged attack on the reformers was having its effect. On the one hand they encouraged the establishment of loyalist associations to counter the effects of the Friends of the

People. On the other they began prosecuting individual reformers for sedition. Thomas Muir was the most important of the reformers to be charged. The delegates of the Edinburgh association met and agreed that they should not use the term 'Friends of the People' in any petition to Parliament 'as this term has become so obnoxious'. A spy reported that the Friends of the People were 'thrown into a state of despondency' by the number of loyalist associations. Some members of the societies, at least in Edinburgh, were in favour of lying low and letting the Government storm pass by. Evidence about country societies indicated that they were less disheartened, but of course less threatened, by the turn of events. At any rate with the morale of the Friends of the People in Edinburgh at a low ebb, Thomas Muir left for London a week after his arrest and arrived on 15 January 1793.

It is not clear what Muir intended to do. He made no secret of his departure, announcing it in public and in the press. He did not hide away in London but was well received by Fox, Grey and other Whig leaders. At a meeting of the Friends of the People in London Muir recounted how he and his friends in Scotland were being persecuted by the agents of the Government. Having taken London reforming circles by storm, at least in his own view, Thomas Muir developed an inflated notion of his own importance. He proposed to exercise his influence in an attempt to help the condemned Louis XVI in Paris. Muir felt that the execution of the French King would jeopardise the reform movement in Britain. Muir may have genuinely believed that he could help Louis XVI but his motive in going to Paris may have been more selfish; Paris was a long way from Edinburgh where in the near future he was to face a charge of sedition.

Before he left London Muir wrote to William Skirving, the secretary of the Edinburgh Convention, to tell him that he would return to Edinburgh to stand trial in three weeks. Muir reached Paris where he failed to save Louis XVI. There were compensations, however, in the welcome he received and his return to Scotland was 'delayed'. 'I am honoured by the notice and friendship of an amiable and distinguished circle', he wrote to his solicitor. Later he wrote again to his solicitor to say that he would return to Scotland when his solicitor thought it was proper –

At the same time, honoured as I am by the civilities and attentions of many amiable characters, it would be with reluctance I could quit Paris for a month or two.

As a lawyer himself Muir must have known that his case was likely to come before the courts sooner than in a month or two. In the same letter he asks to be remembered to his friends. If he were going to see his friends in a month or two such a request seems unnecessary. It could be concluded that Thomas Muir was enjoying the hospitality of the famous men of the French

Revolution whom he greatly admired and had no intention, for the moment at least, of returning to Edinburgh to face his trial for sedition. On 8 February 1793 Muir received word that his trial had been fixed for three days later, 11 February. In the meantime, France had declared war on Britain and Muir could not get passage to Britain whether he wished to or not. He wrote to Edinburgh, explaining his predicament and promising that he would make his way home without delay. The letter was published in the *Edinburgh Gazeteer* on 1 March but by this time Muir had been outlawed for not appearing to answer the charges against him.

Muir's efforts to leave France were protracted. He could not go direct to Britain even if he wished but there were two indirect routes, through Hamburg or via the United States. He argued later during his trial that he had chosen 'the longer, but more certain' route through America because of the war in Europe. His argument may have been justified but the hazards of a transatlantic crossing were considerable. Eventually on 29 April, after nearly three months of French hospitality, Muir got a passport to Philadelphia. Three weeks later he found an American ship at Havre de Grace bound for New York. Although he had paid for a passage on the ship, it was delayed in France for nearly two months. The *Hope* of Baltimore put into Havre de Grace and Muir sailed with her instead.

The *Hope* was due to call at Belfast en route for America. When the ship arrived at Belfast Muir disembarked and went to Dublin where he was fêted by his friends in the United Irishmen. This action belies Muir's claim that he had taken the *Hope* to get back to Scotland more quickly. Muir did something further to confuse the issue of his return to Scotland. While he was in Dublin he asked Captain Towers of the *Hope* to write to his father in Glasgow. The letter, which does not survive, would appear to have been written in guarded terms without reference to Thomas Muir by name at all. It was not a letter from a son announcing his imminent return but one trying to conceal from all but the recipient the fact of Thomas Muir's presence anywhere near Scotland. Furthermore, the reply of Muir's father which was read in court at his trial indicated that he had believed his son was in America, that discreet arrangements had been made to forward his belongings there, and that he now believed that his son was also on the way there. It was also reported in Edinburgh in March and April 1793 that Muir was going to or was already in America. Conclusive evidence is not available, but it seems possible that Muir's reception in Dublin made him change his plans. Thomas Muir was not immune to flattery and the ardent reforming atmosphere of Dublin may have been too much for him. Muir may have felt he should return to Edinburgh to fulfil the role of hero of the Scottish reform movement. There is enough ambiguity about Muir's behaviour in the first six months of 1793 to cast doubt on the accuracy of Muir's own explanations. Early in March, for instance, a spy reported (not necessarily reliably), that Muir had written to friends about his quandary. He was prepared to return and face a large fine but not a prison sentence or transportation.

Muir had arrived in Belfast on or about 17 July. After spending more than a week in Dublin, he returned to Belfast and shortly afterwards, on 30 July 1793, he crossed to Stranraer where he was arrested. When news of his recapture arrived in Edinburgh the Lord Advocate lost no time in getting a warrant for his transmission to Edinburgh. A court messenger was sent to Wigtonshire to escort him back. On 9 August he appeared in court to petition for a recall of sentence of fugitation made against him when he failed to appear for trial. Muir explained his difficulty, sentence was recalled and he was released on bail of 2,000 marks (about £100 sterling).

It has been generally accepted until recently that the trial of Thomas Muir for sedition was a travesty. Writing in the 19th century, for instance, Henry Cockburn, a Whig lawyer involved in the drafting of the 1832 Reform Act (Scotland) said of the trial –

This is one of the cases the memory whereof never perisheth. History cannot let its injustice alone.

Peter MacKenzie, a radical polemicist of the early 19th century, described it as an 'obvious iniquity'. Others have agreed with these assessments. More recently Dr William Ferguson has argued that this view had been based on 'partial history, if not total myth'. It is true that the case of *His Majesty's Advocate against Thomas Muir* was nothing if not a political trial, – 'the real case that was being decided was Burke *contra* Paine.' The jury was packed, the judges were violently partisan, the prosecution's case was circumstantial and based on a self-interested and reactionary political theory; but the defence was mishandled and the defendant himself entered into the spirit of the affair by making political speeches instead of legal defences. The trial of Thomas Muir was a charade played by all the participants including Thomas Muir. That Muir saw himself as a political martyr and his insistence on playing the trial according to the Government's rules led to the fulfilment of that ambition.

The High Court of Justiciary, before which Thomas Muir had to appear, was the highest criminal court in Scotland and from it there was no appeal. The court was presided over and dominated by Robert MacQueen, Lord Braxfield, the Lord Justice-Clerk and highest criminal judge in Scotland. With him on the bench on this occasion were four other judges known as lords commissioner of justiciary, Lords Henderland, Swinton, Dunsinnan and Abercromby. The real Lord Braxfield is not to be confused with the fictional character 'Weir of Hermiston' whom Robert Louis Stevenson undoubtedly based on the notorious presiding judge. Braxfield's conduct of the case was brusque, domineering and by no means impartial. This was his

*Lord Braxfield*

style when hearing all cases and was not specially reserved for sedition trials. He was an experienced judge with a wide knowledge of Scots Law who knew how to temper justice with mercy. Braxfield's behaviour on the bench at the trial of Thomas Muir and at the other sedition trials should not be excused but should be put in perspective. The law on sedition was ill-defined in Scots Law, so that when Braxfield and the other judges could find no law to guide them, they turned to personal and political prejudice.

The trial of Thomas Muir began on 30 August 1793 – a few minutes late because the defendant, whether by accident or design, managed to be late in arriving in court. The proceedings opened, after a reprimand to the panel (the defendant, Thomas Muir) for keeping the court waiting, with the reading of the indictment. The indictment against Thomas Muir fell into four separate charges: wickedly and feloniously exciting by means of seditious speeches and harangues a spirit of disloyalty and disaffection; wickedly and feloniously advising and exhorting persons to purchase and peruse seditious and wicked publications; wickedly and feloniously distributing or circulating seditious writings; and wickedly and feloniously reading seditious writings in public. Muir pleaded Not Guilty and indicated to the court that he would be his own counsel. Henry Erskine, Dean of the Faculty of Advocates and a brilliant defence counsel, had offered to defend him but Muir refused the conditions he laid down. Erskine stipulated that the conduct of the defence should be his alone since he knew that Muir left to himself —

would avow principles and views which would supply the counsel for the Crown with the only thing they wanted to make out their case – *the criminal intention.*

Thomas Muir's first serious mistake in the conduct of his own defence was his failure to challenge the relevancy of the indictment. It was open to him under the rules of criminal procedure to argue before the court that, for instance, even if he had committed the acts alleged in the body of the indictment that they did not amount to the crimes with which he was charged.

The choice of the jury was in the hands of the presiding judge. A list of 45 names was prepared from which Braxfield had to pick 15 jurors. There is strong evidence that the jury lists for all the sedition trials were carefully scrutinised beforehand to ensure that only those well disposed to the Government were included. On this occasion the second person picked by the Lord Justice Clerk was Captain John Inglis of Auchendinny, a naval officer. He felt he could not serve on a jury where the panel was accused of crimes against the Government. The Lord Justice Clerk assured him quite forcibly that there was no impropriety in his serving. When five jurymen had been selected, Muir was asked if he had any objections to those named. He had; all five men were members of the Goldsmiths Hall Association and Muir pointed out that as such they had prejudged the issue before them. The Goldsmiths Hall Association had had the subscription of members of the Society of Friends of the People erased from their books. They could not therefore be impartial in the trial of one of the more prominent members of the Friends of the People. They had also publicly advertised their opposition to the doctrines of Thomas Paine and had offered a reward of 5 guineas to anyone discovering a person circulating his works. Thomas Muir could not expect justice from such a group of men, who had publicly associated to oppose the principles for which he stood. The court repelled Muir's objections to the first five jurymen: he repeated his objection to the second and to the last five and the court repelled those also. Henry Cockburn commented that—

the enpanelling of this jury was virtually the pronouncing of the verdict.

And it is difficult to disagree.

Thirteen witnesses were called by the prosecution but only twelve gave evidence. The thirteenth was the Reverend Mr James Lapslie, minister of Campsie, whom the Lord Advocate withdrew after Muir was able to show that Lapslie had been present when several of the other witnesses had been examined. This was one of Muir's few legal victories during the case. Of the other witnesses four agreed that Muir was indeed an ardent reformer, but one who was also uniformly constitutional in his behaviour. The Lord Advocate was reduced to insinuating that because these, his own witnesses, were also reformers, they were biased. Three further witnesses were called to give evidence about the notorious *Address from the Society of United Irishmen* to the Scottish Convention. They all agreed that Thomas Muir had read it. One witness said that Muir had made no comment on the address thereafter; another thought Muir had said he saw no harm in it; and the third witness remembered that Muir had defended it to the Convention but his defence stopped short of approval. On the evidence of these seven witnesses it can be argued that the Crown had failed to prove its case.

The position is less clear as far as the remaining five witnesses are concerned. The main part of their evidence referred to the charges of recommending and circulating seditious books. Henry Freeland was a weaver and a member of the reform society in Kirkintilloch and Muir was accused of having delivered Paine's *Works* to him. Freeland's evidence, however, indicated that he had mentioned the book to Muir who had said that he thought the book 'had a tendency to mislead weak minds'. When asked if he had a copy of the book, Muir told Freeland that there was a copy in his greatcoat pocket. Freeland then took it from Muir's pocket noting that the pages were uncut. William Muir, another Kirkintilloch weaver, confirmed Freeland's evidence. He also agreed that Muir had given him 11 copies of *The Patriot* to be shown to other members of a reading society. John Muir, a hatter who used to live near Huntershill, admitted that he had bought Paine's *Rights of Man* on Muir's advice. Thomas Muir had asked John Muir if he had read Paine's book. John Muir had not but asked if he could borrow it. Thomas Muir did not have a copy but informed John Muir that he could buy the book. A servant girl was sent out to do so. In the witness box John Muir stated that he would have read the *Rights of Man* anyway but would not have bought it if he could have borrowed it. The fourth of these witnesses was Thomas Wilson, Thomas Muir's barber. He confirmed John Muir's evidence. Further, he stated that in answer to Thomas Muir's question whether he had bought Paine's *Rights of Man* he said he had not. Muir then advised him to buy a copy since a barber's shop was a good place to read. The point was not pressed and Wilson declared that he did not in fact buy the book.

The last of these five witnesses was Anne Fisher, a former servant in the Thomas Muir household. She told the Court that many country people visited Muir's father's shop in the autumn of 1792, that Muir told them often that the *Rights of Man* was a good book, that she had gone and bought it for people in the shop and that she had heard Muir advise Thomas Wilson to buy the *Rights of Man* for his shop. Perhaps most frighteningly of all to the opponents of reform, she said that Muir had sent her to ask a street organist to play *Ca ira*. This tune, the Lord Advocate declared, was used in France 'as a signal for blood and carnage'. When she had finished her evidence, Captain Inglis asked her from the jury-box if she had quarrelled with the Muir family. She said that on the contrary she had been given presents when she left.

The evidence of these five witnesses presents some problems for those who argue that Thomas Muir was simply the innocent victim of a repressive government. The episode with the uncut book in the great-coat pocket is a little odd. There would seem to be grounds for supposing that this was, as the Lord Advocate suggested, a subterfuge. Muir, foreseeing the possibility of action against him by the government, could well have used this ploy in an attempt to avoid subsequent prosecution. The Lord Advocate, on the other hand, cannot be said to have proved his point. It would appear, further, that Muir did advise both John Muir and Thomas Wilson to buy Paine's *Rights of Man*. If Anne Fisher is to be believed he advised many others to do so also. This tends to indicate that Muir was guilty of the second charge in the indictment although, again, it is not conclusive. Anne Fisher gave the most damning and precise evidence against Muir. The question is – is she to be believed? The answer suggested by one pro-Muir polemicist is that at the time of the trial Anne Fisher was employed by a government appointee who bought her testimony on their behalf. She was also believed by that writer to have later become a prostitute. It is possible that Fisher was bribed and coached in her evidence. She was, perhaps, more detailed and precise about events which took place a year previously than can be credited. On the other hand, if that was so, why did Thomas Muir not submit her to a searching cross-examination? He said that he would not deign to question 'such a witness'. This may have simply been another of Muir's tactical errors but one is left with the possibility that he did not dare cross-examine because he knew what she said to be true.

Taken together the evidence against Muir was not substantial and on very few points did it support the spirit of the indictment. The defence witnesses whom Muir called, naturally, supported his contention that he had always acted within the constitution. According to his witnesses his views were those of a constitutionalist who wished to see certain abuses removed and the constitution restored to its former vigour. Some of the evidence related to his absence in France and his efforts to keep in touch with Edinburgh. Throughout he was represented as a man who always urged moderation, who never incited riot, who never circulated or recommended the books mentioned in the indictment and who was particularly critical of the works of Thomas Paine. The Lord Advocate rarely cross-examined Muir's witnesses and in summing up said nothing against them except that they too were reformers. After the 21st defence witness had been heard, Muir stated that many more could be called but that he thought he had made his point.

While the Lord Advocate's address was an uninspired appeal to the jury's most paranoid feelings about reform, Muir's address was powerful and eloquent. His speech lifted the trial from the level of mediocrity that went before. Without it perhaps Muir would not be remembered today. If Thomas Muir had deliberately chosen political martyrdom then the opportunity to make this speech was what he had been waiting for. If his conduct of the case had been less than skilful his closing speech was masterly. If he had hoped for an acquittal, however, his speech put paid to this optimism. In the course of his speech he explained his absence in France, denying that it was consciousness of his guilt that kept him there. He argued about the nature of the crime of sedition – 'a term so vague and so undefined, so familiar to power, so familiar to corruption' – but he did so at the wrong time. It was now too late. He tried to show that his views on the reform of the constitution were consistent with those of other accepted commentators and politicians including Locke, Blackstone, the Duke of Richmond, William Pitt and even Robert Dundas, the Lord Advocate, his prosecutor. He accepted he was in court because he was a reformer.

If the real cause of my standing as a panel at your bar, is for actively engaging in the cause of a parliamentary reform, I plead guilty.

Muir concluded that the Crown had failed to prove its case and that he should be acquitted. In his final stirring sentences he stated his continuing adherence to the cause of reform.

It is a good cause; It shall ultimately prevail – It shall finally triumph.

When he sat down there was a spontaneous and almost unanimous burst of applause.

It was now after midnight on the morning of 31 August. Lord Braxfield began his charge to the jury. The question, he said, for them to consider was simple: on the evidence, was the panel guilty of sedition? There were two points on which no proof was required; firstly the British Constitution was the best in the world; secondly there was a spirit of sedition and revolt abroad during the winter months of 1792–93. He wondered if it was entirely innocent of Muir to talk of reform among 'ignorant country people' and 'among the lower classes of the people'. Muir should have known that no attention would be paid by Parliament 'to such a rabble'. Braxfield's conception of the basis of Government was simplicity itself –

A Government in every country should be just like a Corporation, and in this country it is made up of the landed interest which alone has a right to be represented. As for the rabble, who have nothing but personal property, what hold has the nation of them?

The Lord Justice Clerk concluded his address by stating his own belief in the panel's guilt and urging the Jury 'to return such verdict as would do them honour'. It was half past one in the morning. The Court was adjourned till noon and the jury 'enclosed' until then.

When the Court met again the jury returned the unanimous and inevitable verdict – 'Guilty of the crimes libelled'. Before consulting the other judges as to the appropriate sentence, Braxfield thanked the jury and informed the members that the Court 'highly approved of the verdict they had given' – an unprecedented step. In the opinion of Lord Henderland, there were five possibilities for Muir's sentence – banishment, fine, whipping, imprisonment or transportation. Banishment would only send a dangerous man to another country, which probably meant England. A fine would fall on Muir's unfortunate parents while whipping was too disgraceful especially for a man of 'his character and rank of life'. Imprisonment was only temporary; that left transportation – the only suitable punishment according to Lord Henderland. Lord Swinton saw little distinction between Muir's crime and treason. He felt no punishment for Muir's crime was adequate 'now that torture is happily abolished' but reluctantly concluded that transportation for 14 years would suffice as a punishment. Lords Dunsinnan and Abercomby concurred. Lord Braxfield's only doubt about the sentence was whether transportation should be for life or for 14 years. The 'indecent applause' that had greeted Muir's address to the jury had convinced Braxfield that 'a spirit of discontent still lurked in the minds of the people' and that it would be dangerous to allow Muir any possibility of returning to Scotland. Finally Lord Braxfield agreed with his colleagues and Thomas Muir was sentenced to be transported to Botany Bay for a period of 14 years on pain of death if he returned to any part of Great Britain.

Muir's immediate reaction was calm –

I have engaged in a good, a just and a glorious cause – a cause which sooner or later, must and will prevail, and by timely reform save this country from destruction.

As early as February 1793, while he was in France, we have seen that he feared the possibility of transportation; now that fear had been realised. The

*Tolbooth in Edinburgh*

jury was as shocked at the sentence as Muir. Some of the jury members apparently believed that a few weeks' imprisonment, or at most a few months, would have been sufficient. The jury members met the day after the trial to discuss what they should do. At the meeting Gilbert Innes of Stow, their foreman, produced a letter with a threat to assassinate him for finding Muir guilty. The jury then felt it impossible to proceed since it might appear they were yielding to the threat. Other members of the jury later received threatening letters.

Efforts were made by Muir's supporters to show that the High Court of Justiciary had no powers to transport for sedition. Such arguments the Court simply rebutted. In fact, the punishment of transportation itself was probably illegal. The Act empowering transportation of offenders had expired in 1788 and Scotland had been omitted when it was renewed. At the time, however, no one picked up this technicality. Although a few Whigs tried to pursue the matter in Parliament, the Government and the Court of Justiciary would not be budged.

The prosecuting and sentencing of Thomas Muir failed to bring an end to the political reform movement in Scotland, if that had been the Government's intention. The only success was in frightening off many of the more 'respectable' reformers. In September 1793, it was reported that the Friends

*Convict hulk in the Thames*

of the People had been revived by Muir's sentence. Handbills against the sentence and against the Government appeared in Edinburgh. Rumour had it that Muir was to be rescued from the Tolbooth and the magistrates of Edinburgh were very anxious that he should be moved to London as soon as possible. In defiance of the Government, the Friends of the People contemplated holding another General Convention, which met at the end of October, and sent invitations to delegates from England. The English delegates did not arrive until after the Convention was adjourned but, on its recall, the Convention renamed itself 'The British Convention of Delegates of the People associated for obtaining Universal Suffrage and annual Parliaments'. The Government's action in staging the political trial of Thomas Muir (and later that of T. F. Palmer) resulted in the revival of the Friends of the People, not its demise. The revived Friends of the People was a more radical organisation and it had closer links with the English movement. It was, however, short-lived. The British Convention was broken up on 5 December 1793 by the Lord Provost of Edinburgh and 30 constables. Despite efforts to ensure its survival after this severe setback, subsequent political reforming activity in Scotland was driven underground for over twenty years. More political trials followed the dispersal of the British Convention. Maurice Margarot and Joseph Gerrald, delegates from the London Corresponding Society, and William Skirving, secretary to the Convention, were each sentenced to 14 years' transportation.

At the end of November 1793 Muir and Palmer had been shipped from the Forth to the Thames to wait for a suitable transport to Australia. Muir's spirits had remained high while in Edinburgh until he was given notice of his departure. In the hulks and in Newgate, every day brought home to him the reality and hopelessness of his position. His health suffered; he had rheumatism and showed early signs of consumption. Margarot and Skirving joined their colleagues in the Thames but Gerrald's trial was postponed so that he did not come south from Edinburgh until after the others had left. Muir and the others set sail for New South Wales on 2 May 1794. On the long voyage Muir kept himself to himself. He suffered severe bouts of melancholy, he apparently took to drink and may have become involved with one of the women convicts. Palmer and Skirving took part in an attempted mutiny and spent the latter part of the voyage in partial confinement. Margarot became friendly with the ship's captain and finished the voyage in some comfort. It was an estranged group which reached Botany Bay on 25 October after a voyage of six months.

None of the reformers arrived at the other side of the world without private means of support. Palmer and two free settlers, Ellis and Boston, founded a trading and manufacturing company. Thomas Muir settled for 30 acres of land about 2 miles from the main settlement. He named it

'Huntershill'. He had a house in the settlement and was allowed two convicts as servants. He owned a boat and was permitted to fish. In 1795 John Boston successfully sued one of the military garrison for assault and Muir may have assisted in the case. He may also have gone into the printing business but whatever the distractions, life in the penal colony was bleak. In 1795 Muir wrote to friends in London that—

their rememberance is the only idea that disturbs the repose of my tomb, for so I might call this situation of privation from all that is dear to me.

The dullness and hopelessness of the situation changed dramatically when the *Otter*, a ship from Boston captained by Ebenezer Dow, arrived in Sydney Cove on 24 January 1796. The ship was on a trading mission to China. It had not been, as has been claimed, specially fitted out by George Washington to rescue Thomas Muir – but rescue him it did. François Peron, the first mate, heard of Muir's career and agreed to help him escape. Captain Dow was less enthusiastic but he was short of crew and had intended taking some convicts anyway, so he finally agreed to take Muir.

The *Otter* sailed east across the Pacific, passing Tonga, until in May 1796 she arrived off the North West coast of America. At Nootka Sound they were joined by the Spanish ship, the *Sutil*, which was checking on the movements of British and American ships. Muir transferred himself and his baggage – which was considerable for a man on the run – from the *Otter* to the *Sutil* before the ships left Nootka. He did so for a combination of reasons. He wanted to go south where the *Sutil* was headed, he wanted to avoid a British vessel, *HMS Providence*, which was also in the area and he certainly did not want to go to China which was the *Otter*'s destination. Muir and the *Sutil* were driven south to Monterey where he remained for some weeks, writing letters to the United States from where he hoped they might reach his friends and relations at home. From Monterey he was sent on to San Blas in Mexico, escorted to Vera Cruz and then went by sea to Havannah, Cuba. He arrived there on 19 November 1796.

Until his arrival in Havannah he had been treated as an honoured guest although some of his hosts were a little uneasy that such a figure should be at large in New Spain. In Havannah unease became hostility and Muir was imprisoned there for four months because Britain and Spain were now at war. Muir's hopes of getting to the United States were shattered. Instead he found himself in March 1797 aboard the Spanish frigate, *Ninfa*, bound for Cadiz. When in sight of her destination, the *Ninfa* was intercepted by a British force under Sir John Jervis. Muir was severely wounded in the ensuing fight; he was injured in the face and lost his left eye. He was not recognised by the British, who had somehow found out he was aboard, because of his mutilation. The story is told that he was in fact recognised by the British naval surgeon who had been at school with him but who allowed him to be sent ashore with the wounded. At any rate Muir found himself ashore in Cadiz where the French consul saw to his comfort. The French Government, the Directory, demanded that Spain release him and in November 1797, after a long convalescence, he was allowed to travel to France.

He arrived in Bordeaux to scenes of jubilation. He then went to Paris where his arrival was heralded by a eulogistic account of his life by David in *Le Moniteur Universal*. The Directory provided him with funds for his support and Muir soon entered into the life of Paris, basking in the adulation that at first surrounded him. Two Scots merchants, Benjamin and John Sword, described to the authorities in Edinburgh, how they had met Thomas Paine and Thomas Muir while on an (illegal) visit to Paris. Muir had got drunk and argued with Paine about religion. The Swords got the impression that Muir lived well, and for a time he did. In order to make himself useful, he wrote articles on the state of England and Scotland. England, he said was not ready for invasion, the lower classes there would not welcome the French. In Scotland, however, the people, because of their superior moral character and their awareness of politics, were ready to give such an invasion their support. Muir also worked with Napper Tandy publishing articles on behalf of the United Irishmen. Like so many political exiles, the United Irishmen in Paris had split into factions. Tandy had tried to smear his colleagues, including the founder of the movement Wolfe Tone. In collaborating with Tandy, Muir claimed to have the authority of the movement in Ireland when he put their case to the French press. This did not endear him to men like Tone. By May 1798 Muir had begun to run short of money. He appealed to the Directory for help, offering to sell them his memoirs in return for a small estate. His request lay in the ministry concerned until after his death, and the document bears the poignant marginal note 'Since then Muir has died'. His health, eroded by the privations of his circumnavigation and ruined by the injuries he received at Cadiz, deteriorated further. He died, alone and unknown, on 26 January 1799, in the little town of Chantilly.

Thomas Muir was an important leader of the movement for parliamentary reform in Scotland and one of the five 'political martyrs' in that cause. He has gained that reputation because of his trial for sedition at the hands of a repressive government and because of the eloquent and moving speech made in his own defence at the end of the trial. He was not a great theorist nor a great writer. There were flaws in his character which at times threatened to deny him a prominent place in the history of the reform movement. Doubts still exist about his motives at crucial points in his career. He did, however, take the ideas of reform to the ordinary people, the weavers of the Campsie villages, and he took a leading part in the popular and democratic Friends of the People, dedicated to equal electoral representation and shorter parliaments. One of his greatest crimes in the eyes of the establishment was introducing these ideas to working people. His greatest contribution to the reform movement was in doing so and then simply and clearly in his trial publicly avowing these principles. In the circumstances, this was a brave thing to do.

As an individual Muir was not always easy to get on with. Two contemporaries had this to say of him. Archibald Fletcher, leader of the Scottish burgh reformers, commented of Muir:

I believe him to be an honest enthusiast, but he is an ill-judging man.

Wolfe Tone, the United Irishmen's leader whom Muir had annoyed, wrote of him in 1798,

Of all the vain, obstinate blockheads that I ever met, I never saw his equal.

Henry Cockburn, writing over thirty years after his death, is less harsh in his judgement,

distinguished by no superiority of talent, he was . . . a man of ordinary sense.

In the end, all that can be said of Thomas Muir is that he was a man who developed a commitment to the idea of parliamentary reform. He took up the task of promoting reform enthusiastically and suffered as a result. His trial shows how much in need of reform was the government and parliament of Britain at the end of the eighteenth century.

# Patrick Sellar

## Ian Grimble

It is a brave historian who ignores legends, an unwary one who tries to debunk them. History is the evidence of contemporary documents, generally compiled by the ruling administration, often fabricated by the victors in a conflict, frequently subjected to the suppression of unattractive details. Legend is the transmitted experience of people at the receiving end of history, often preserved in a language unrecognised by the rulers, most conveniently memorised in verse. Complicated issues tend to be personalised by heroes and villains in a manner easily faulted for over-simplification and factual inaccuracy. Yet some people believe that a legend is capable of enshrining profound truths of past human experience as well as the most impeccably documented history, and the case of Patrick Sellar possesses all the features that enable us to decide whether they are right or wrong.

Had he lived in a more remote age the legends surrounding him would probably have ceased to generate academic heat: just as people can enjoy the English ballads of Robin Hood, although French-speaking bishops and sheriffs of the Middle Ages would not have approved of them; understanding as we now do the underlying causes that gave them such an important place in folk memory. But Sellar died as recently as 1851 and today Gaelic traditions concerning him are still locked in conflict with historical judgement. In 1968 Dr Phillip Gaskell wrote of 'the absurdity of the Sellar folk-lore which still persists in Scotland'. He described *The Trial of Patrick Sellar* (I. Grimble, 1962) as an 'attack' on Sellar, and was presumably defining this odd term when he spoke of unnamed 'popular historians who have been interested chiefly in the propagandist or sentimental aspects of the subject'. The theme, in fact, is capable of inspiring historians to explore one another's motives, not merely their arguments.

In 1969 Dr T. C. Smout praised Dr Gaskell as 'cool-headed', and described the author of *The Trial of Patrick Sellar* as 'thick with passion but thin on research'. Whether by design or accident, this verdict goes to the heart of the matter. The passion was that of the people whose lives were so deeply affected by Sellar's career, expressed in the only manner open to them. If their passion was misconceived it should have been possible for the administration he served to provide from its muniments the documentary evidence to prove this. Yet the book in question was 'thin on research' because an application to examine these muniments was refused. They have been withheld subsequently from the most eminent historian in this field, Dr Eric Richards, who

*Patrick Sellar*

has commented on these archives of the house of Sutherland at Dunrobin castle: 'it is almost as if the Dunrobin manuscripts have been subject to an attentuated "150-year rule" by which the world of scholarship received instalments of documents at certain spaced intervals.'

Access to them has been restricted for decades to a single scholar who is the son of the late factor to the late Duke of Sutherland, so that a vast body of evidence that might have been exposed to public scrutiny with the assistance of a team of archivists is diminished to a trickle selected by one individual. It would be hard to find any comparable example of such a phenomenon in the field of European scholarship, and it is an important aspect of the Sellar case, dominating whatever is written about it from year to year.

Patrick Sellar was brought to trial in Inverness in 1816 on charges of inhumanity in the discharge of his duties as a factor of Elizabeth, Countess of Sutherland in her own right, and Marchioness of Stafford by marriage. Two years previously Sellar had obtained a huge sheep farm for himself in the Naver valley but before he could take possession the twenty-seven sub-tenants, their families, dependants and cottars had to be evicted. When Sellar and his men rode into Strathnaver on Monday, 13 June 1814, to clear the glen they expected little opposition and there was none, but their manner and methods of removal together with some tragic consequences resulted in Sellar being accused of excessive cruelty, wilful fire-raising, throwing down buildings and endangering lives. Many impartial people have believed from that day to this that he was justly acquitted by the jury, and indeed, at the conclusion of the trial the judge addressed him as follows: 'Mr Sellar, it is now my duty to dismiss you from the bar; and you have the satisfaction of thinking that you are discharged by the unanimous opinion of the Jury and Court. I am sure that, although your feelings must have been agitated, you cannot regret that this trial took place; and I am hopeful it will have due effect on the minds of the country, which have been so much and so improperly agitated.'

The effect proved to be very different from the one for which Lord Pitmilly hoped, as a Gaelic poem composed soon after the verdict became known makes abundantly clear.

Sellar is in Culmaily
Left there like a wolf
Seizing and oppressing
All that comes within his reach.
It is a disaster you were not put in prison
For years on bread and water
And a hard loop of iron
Firmly, securely round your thigh.

And a century after his death the people of Sutherland still sing in Gaelic:

> Sellar, you are in your grave,
> The lamentation of widows in your ears.
> The perdition you brought upon the people,
> Since then you have had your own fill of it.[1]

Whatever the historical truth about the career of Patrick Sellar, he has become a legendary ogre like Guy Fawkes in England, unredeemed by time or the corrective judgments of scholars.

An interesting aspect of this is that he cannot be said to have been victimised by the principle that folk-lore abhors a vacuum. The Scottish Highlands were haunted before he was born by a monster of such horrifying aspect that demonologists had no need to seek another. The cruelties committed by Butcher Cumberland after the battle of Culloden in 1746 were still a living memory when the new century opened.

On the other hand, the people of Sutherland had not suffered from the excesses of the Duke of Cumberland: indeed they had passed virtually unscathed through every vicissitude of the Jacobite era. The two magnates who owned most of the county, Lord Reay, Chief of Mackay and the Earl of Sutherland had supported the Protestant revolution of 1688 that turned James VII off his throne; and they had adopted the Hanoverian cause in the uprisings of 1715 and 1745. Remote from the centres of government, the archaic way of life of their patriarchal world had continued with relatively little disturbance, apart from the annoyance of the proscription of Highland dress, the abolition of local jurisdictions and the Disarming Act, which were imposed on loyal and disloyal clans alike.

The most numerous clan in Sutherland county were the Mackays, who had once possessed an entire territory bounded by the north coast from Cape Wrath to the Caithness border, and divided from the Sutherland earldom to its south by an underbelly of hills of which the massif of Ben Klibreck and Ben Armine were to acquire particular significance in the Sellar story. Beneath them lies Loch Naver and from it the river of that name flows north through the heart of the Mackay province that was named Strathnaver after it. By the 18th century the ownership of the Naver valley had passed to the Earls of Sutherland, so that the Mackays lived partly under their rule, partly under Mackay Chiefs and junior branches of their family in the lands either side of the Naver valley. Many other Highland names had been settled in the province of Strathnaver, but that of its original clan remained so predominant that it was still known as *Duthaich 'Ic Aoidh* – the Mackay Country – then, and to this day.

It was the good fortune of the Mackays that their way of life was depicted from within by Rob Donn the bard (1714–78) in the most comprehensive and detailed body of social poetry that was ever composed in the eighteenth-century Highlands. It is worth all the comments of outside observers put together, and confirmed by them at many significant points. For instance one of these wrote in 1750: 'the common people of the Mackays are the most religious of all the tribes that dwell among the mountains, south or north.'

The Mackays also possessed an outstanding military tradition, dating back to the time when the first Lord Reay had taken his personal regiment to fight in the Thirty Years' War in 1628. Since then Mackays had played a prominent part in maintaining the Scots Brigade in the Protestant Netherlands, supplying it with officers and also filling its ranks with soldiers for limited periods of service. 'The Mackays are said to be a better militia than any of the neighbouring clans, for which this is assigned as a reason,' wrote the same anonymous observer in 1750. Their combination of piety and discipline was the subject of intermittent comment wherever they went.

They contributed conspicuously to the regiment that the Earl of Sutherland raised in 1759, and such was their response to the recruiting drives of the ensuing decades that a tacksman wrote from Durness to one of Lord Reay's factors in 1798: 'I think they must see little who does not see this country approaching rapidly into a state of *depopulation*, and that by the very means once thought favourable, I mean the volunteer establishments. Such effect has the smattering of exercise upon the rising generation, aided by their pay, which is all converted to dissipation, that not one individual able to lift a drumstick now remains unenlisted in Durness. And I'm told the case is pretty similar in other parts of this estate, though not quite so bad.' From then until the end of the Napoleonic War in 1815 the drain continued. However, the overall population of Sutherland did not fall during these years. It rose from 20,774 in 1755 to 23,117 in 1801. The introduction of small-pox vaccination contributed to this, while the adoption of potato-growing helped to feed the increasing numbers.

People lived by cattle husbandry supplemented by agriculture so far as the land allowed. It was a frugal existence as Bishop Pococke found on his visit to Sutherland in 1760. 'The people live very hardy,' he wrote from Tongue, 'principally on milk, curds, whey, and a little oatmeal, especially when they are at the sheals in the mountain, that is, cabins or huts in which they live when they go to the mountains with their cattle during the months of June, July and August. Their best food is oat or barley cakes. A porridge made of oatmeal, cale and sometimes a piece of salt meat in it, is the top fare. Except that by the sea they have plenty of fish in summer, and yet they will hardly be at the pains of catching it but in very fine weather. . . . The people are in general extremely hospitable, charitable, civil, polite and sensible.'

Their cattle were dowry and bank balance; only to a very limited extent the food of the poorest. The marketing of the beasts was conducted by droving expeditions to the great cattle fairs of the south, managed largely by the tacksmen or leaseholders, that middle rank in clan society which was to disappear to a considerable extent in the lifetime of Patrick Sellar. While the economy was hit periodically by the hazardous climate of the northern mainland, the continuous rise in the price of cattle throughout the latter half of the eighteenth century helped to preserve it from being undermined by external forces.

But the society of Sutherland possessed an inherent internal weakness. Unlike the peoples who lived in a comparable environment and latitude in Scandinavia, it did not consist of a free peasantry possessing security of tenure in its small-holdings and hill pastures. On the contrary, their condition more closely resembled that of the Russian serfs, in that the majority enjoyed access to the means of subsistence at the mere will of their landlords, and this might be made conditional upon the performance of arbitrary and unlimited services, and also of their joining the army when required to do so. The insecurity was softened, however, by the kindly relationships that survived in a clan hierarchy relatively undisturbed by the social, political and economic forces that had affected other parts of the Highlands. It was generally believed that the Chief would respect customary rights which were supposed to have existed since remote times: Lord Pitmilly himself gave weight to 'a customary right' which Sellar was alleged at his trial to have contravened. And a conviction also lingered throughout the Highlands that a Chief held his property in trust for his clansmen, as the common property of them all, even though they possessed no legal titles.

These flimsy alternatives to peasant proprietorship were gradually eroded as landlords acquired an increasing taste for metropolitan life and drained capital out of their estates to spend abroad. More significant than an uncertain climate, the rise in population or economic trends was the question whether the tribal father continued to live among his people, fulfilling his unwritten obligations to them, or regarded them simply as his personal capital, to be squandered elsewhere.

When the fifth Lord Reay died in 1768, he was succeeded by an idiot brother in whose name the property was managed by trustees. By lucky chance the idiot outlived the collateral heir, so that the estate was not required to feed the extravagances of this notoriously irresponsible man. But in 1797 it passed instead to his son, who proved to be equally improvident, with results that form part of the Sellar story.

A comparable disaster struck the Sutherland earldom. A popular young Earl and Countess died in 1766 leaving only a baby daughter Elizabeth, whose title to be Countess was contested by male collaterals of her family. After an expensive lawsuit her case was won in 1771, when Rob Donn expressed his optimism for the future.

> I was likening the Chieftains
> To a good oven that was useful
> After its fire was extinguished
> And when only an ember remained.
> O I am confident yet
> That in a little time from now
> That spark Betty will
> Blaze into a joyous fire.[2]

But long before the young Countess visited her earldom for the first time, the effects of absentee landlordism were being experienced there by her people. She was brought up in Edinburgh by her Lowland grandmother while agents descended upon her estate to extract from it the considerable cost of her maintenance: and as in all parts of the world where this system has operated, they enriched themselves at the same time.

'The evil is the greater,' deposed one of their victims, 'that the estate being parcelled out to different factors and tacksmen, these must oppress the sub-tenants in order to raise a profit to themselves, particularly on the article of cattle, which they never fail to take at their own prices, lately 20 shillings or 20 merks, and seldom or never higher than 30 shillings, though the same cattle have been sold in the country from 50 to 55 shillings.' Another complained of the 'oppressive services exacted by the factor, being obliged to work with his people and cattle for forty days and more each year, without a bit of bread'. At the same time their rents were increased: in some cases they were more than doubled.

It was a period of massive emigration from the Highlands to America, and this testimony, amply supported by others, was given by men from the Sutherland estate. The exodus reached its peak in 1774, until it was arrested by the outbreak of the American War of Independence in the following year. The contributory causes were generally common to all areas, though in varying degrees. In the Hebrides the population rise seems to have been far steeper than in Sutherland, while the effects of plenty or food shortage might exert a very local influence. For instance, the Minister of Reay on the border between Sutherland and Caithness wrote in 1774: 'The price of victual is falling daily. Demands from the south are but slow, and the crop in the Highlands was last year so plentiful that very little will be bought by the Highland lairds.' Similarly, the conduct of landlords varied. Others were criticised at least as harshly as the managers of the Sutherland estate, while there were those who neither deserved nor received such condemnation.

Suffice to say that whatever the general causes of this widespread emigration, the explicit testimony of people from Sutherland, amplified by Lowland journalists who questioned folk as they journeyed south to sail in the emigrant ships, points to a particular cause of discontent there. It is confirmed by a poem composed by Donald Matheson, the religious poet of Kildonan, surprisingly, since he did not discuss secular matters in verse as a rule. His Biblical parallel for what he witnessed is about as devastating an indictment as could be imagined.

> I am seeing the shadow
> Of things that happened long ago,
> When the people of Israel were
> In distress in Egypt.
> He took them with a strong hand
> Away from Pharoah himself,
> And he divided the sea for them
> When Pharoah hastened after them.[3]

The managers of the Sutherland estate, in fact, were opposed to emigration; neither did they care for the publicity attending it. 'Our emigrants made very false report in regard to the cause of their leaving the country,' one complained, while Matheson observed:

> I am seeing hardships
> Now on every hand,
> Families that were respectable
> With their heads brought low,
> Servants in the role of landlords
> And young children as heirs,
> The land full of distress –
> O God, who can endure it?[3]

By fortunate chance Sutherland was visited in 1772 by the naturalist and antiquarian Thomas Pennant, whose comments provide a remarkable contrast to those of Bishop Pococke just over a decade earlier. They appear to refer exclusively to a region administered by the managers of the young Countess, and they add significantly to the pictures drawn by emigrant, poet and journalist. '*This tract seems the residence of sloth;*' wrote Pennant, '*the people* almost torpid with idleness, and most wretched: their hovels most miserable, made of poles wattled and covered with thin sods. There is not corn raised sufficient to supply half the wants of the inhabitants: *climate conspires with indolence to make matters worse*; yet there is much improvable land here in a state of nature: but till famine pinches they will not bestir themselves: *they are content with little at present, and are thoughtless of futurity; perhaps on the motive of Turkish vassals, who are oppressed in proportion to their improvements. Dispirited and driven to despair by bad management, crowds are now passing, emaciated with hunger, to the Eastern coast, on the report of a ship being loaden with meal.* Numbers of the miserables of this country were now migrating: they wandered in a state of desperation; too poor to pay, they madly sell themselves for their passage, prefering a temporary bondage in a strange land to starving for life in their native soil.'

Commenting on the events of Patrick Sellar's lifetime, Dr Smout emphasised the need to explore this background in his *History of the Scottish People*, 1969, and he quoted that passage from Pennant, omitting the parts that have been placed here in italics. For after the visitation of Patrick Sellar people were apt to look back to a golden age, which Dr Smout identifies as one of the myths, comparing Pennant's harsh picture with some nostalgic writings of the mid-nineteenth century. 'Sutherland had never been,' wrote Dr Smout, 'a peasant Arcadia of rosy prosperity, plump girls and happy bakers.'

On the contrary, the five hundred pages of Rob Donn's contemporary Gaelic poetry contain many plump girls and happy bakers, frequent glimpses of Arcadia: they cannot be dismissed like a nineteenth-century tract. Furthermore the evidence of emigrants written down in 1774 agrees with Donald Matheson that people had become demoralised by recent oppression, 'families that were respectable with their heads brought low'. Pennant observed the cause in a passage missing from Dr Smout's quotation, just as all the other contemporary evidence is missing from his book which lends support to the legend he wishes to dismiss. It is indeed essential, as he insists, to explore the background to the conflict between the legend of Patrick Sellar and the interpretations of historians, for its roots lie deep.

Many people in Sutherland, remembering a happier past, must have shared Rob Donn's confidence that the emergency would end once that spark Betty had blazed into a joyous fire.

She married an Englishman who succeeded to an immense fortune and to the title of Marquess of Stafford in 1803. He was described as 'a dull, nervous man', while his wife possessed a vitality and intelligence that were inherited by their son, Earl Gower. She took seriously her position as *Ban Mhorair Cataibh*, the Chieftainess of Sutherland, and so did her son who was heir to the Chiefship as well as to so much else. Before 1803 the revenues of Sutherland were drained from their property for the family's support, but after that date they were able to discuss the possibilities of massive investment in Sutherland for the benefit of its inhabitants as well as their own. In London the Countess liked to keep Gaelic servants dressed in the fanciful Highland costume of the period, but her correspondence proves that *La petite reine barbare* was not simply concerned with the romantic trappings of her position. On the contrary, it reveals that she possessed the genuine concern, combined with the autocratic attitude, of a Catherine the Great.

*opposite page, Elizabeth Gordon, Countess of Sutherland*

She exemplified both in 1799 when she learned that her clansmen were responding without enthusiasm to a call to the colours from her cousin General Wemyss. He considered withdrawing from the campaign of recruitment, and the Countess wrote to her factor John Fraser: 'I would have him do it, or at least threaten to do it if they do not come in in a certain time, as they are really unworthy of his attention, and need no longer be considered as a credit to Sutherland or any advantage *over sheep* or any other useful animal.' Her clansmen proved to be useful animals after all, filling the 93rd Regiment of Sutherland Highlanders in what was to prove the last of the clan levies, fighting with outstanding bravery, and doubtless supposing that they had protected their folk from being evicted in favour of sheep. An estate document of 1806 reveals how rigorously their private obligation to a tribal Chieftainess in nineteenth-century Britain was enforced. A black-list had been kept of 'tenants in Kildonan who thought proper in the course of the recruiting to show a preference of other Regiments to the two which the Marquis and Marchioness recommended'. Those who had acted with total subservience might reasonably assume that the obligation was a reciprocal one.

It was in the year 1806 that the first large-scale improvement was begun, designed to modernise the economic structure of Sutherland. The most generally approved policy of the time was to gather a scattered tenantry into villages, preferably on the coast where they would be able to pursue the dual occupations of crofter-fishermen, while the inland valleys and hill pastures were divided into sheep farms. It was recognised that such a reorganisation would arouse opposition amongst a conservative population, but there is not reason to doubt the good faith of the Countess and her amenable husband in the magnanimity of their intentions, despite her petulant remark during the recruitment campaign of 1799.

The very first experiment, however, revealed the gulf that may yawn between a good intention and its implementation. In 1806 Adam Atkinson and Anthony Marshall, sheep farmers from Northumberland, offered a rental three times as high as the land had yielded previously for a property that lay beneath Ben Klibreck and Ben Armine, overlooking the Naver valley. A second area near Lairg was given over to sheep in 1808. The Countess evidently believed that adequate arrangements had been made for the resettlement of the people cleared from these areas, for she wrote to her husband on 27 July in that year: 'all those dismissed from Lairg are already settled.' How wrong she was is revealed by the fact that three hundred people were moved two days later: and more serious still, they were not rehoused on the coast where they might have taken up fishing, nor given adequate land for the crops and cattle. They were simply unloaded on the communities of other small tenants further along the banks of Loch Naver, at Gnub Mór, Gnub Beag and Achness where there was scarcely room for them.

Already the Countess was being 'very much abused for turning off last year a great number of small tenants who had held land under the family for upwards of two hundred years, and making sheep farms'. It was a sympathetic friend who said this, and she added, 'I doubt whether in a few years they will not feel the advantage of this new plan.' But in fact those over-crowded communities awaited still more drastic treatment at the hands of Patrick Sellar in the following decade. In the meantime many of the young men in them went away to seek work, as someone informed the son of the Countess in 1810, mentioning incidentally that they were of excellent character. 'They honestly admitted that it was necessity which drove them from home and that they cannot live without going in search of work since the numbers of people have been so much increased by those sent down among them when Marshall and Atkinson got the sheep farm.'

The informant's name was William Young, and he obtained employment from the Countess in the following circumstances. Across the waters of the firth from Dunrobin castle he had improved some of the coastal lands of Moray, and had also built a fishing village at Hopeman, with a harbour from which corn and lime could be exported and coal unloaded. In 1809 he visited Sutherland in the company of a young lawyer named Patrick Sellar, who had just joined a business consortium of which Young was the head.

Sellar was the son of an Edinburgh-trained lawyer who had come to practise his profession in Moray and there made a notably successful career for himself. In particular, he had improved an impoverished estate for one of his clients, and purchased it in 1808. When his son Patrick came to Sutherland in the following year they saw the opportunity to do the same on the 300 acre farm of Culmaily, near to Dunrobin, and offered to take a lease of it. It was natural that the Countess should welcome such promising exponents of her own plans for the future, especially when they were approved by George Macpherson Grant of Ballindalloch, who became Member of Parliament for Sutherland in 1809. 'I had a letter from Macpherson Grant,' she told her son, 'recommending these people strongly as the greatest advantage to the carrying on our future plans of improvement, getting settlers from Moray, and settling our own people as villagers.'

Into her receptive ears these two confident young men, who had never visited Sutherland before and knew virtually nothing of its climate, soil, nor of its peculiar social and economic structure, poured advice for its improvement ranging far beyond the lands of Culmaily. They undermined her confidence in the present Commissioner of her estates, Cosmo Falconer, rightly pointing out how in the previous removals people had been crammed into hamlets 'without *any new tract being pointed out for their industry*, and wanting, we fear, the full supply they formerly enjoyed on their boundless pastures – depression, debility, sloth, filth, are the consequences – disease follows;

contagion spreads; and where all are predestinarians careless of precaution, and little aid is to be procured, it is not wonderful that much mischief is done'.

For her part, the Countess pronounced Falconer ignorant equally 'of Turnips or Mankind' and in 1810 she offered his post to William Young, with Patrick Sellar as his assistant. To Sir Walter Scott she wrote: 'I have great hopes at present from the abilities of this Mr Young, of considerable improvements being effected in Sutherland and without routing and destroying the old inhabitants, which contrary to the Theories respecting these matters, I am convinced is very possible.' Her motives appear beyond reproach: it only remained to be seen how theory would be matched by practice.

When Falconer heard that he was to be replaced, he wrote to the Marquess of Stafford a dignified letter of warning. 'With regard to my successors they have shewn themselves to be men of enterprise in their own concerns and one of them I am sure had disinterestedly shown zeal for the improvement of the country.' But he had already formed a very different opinion of Patrick Sellar. 'The other a raw inexperienced young man could, with great submission, have no claim to the honour your Lordship and family have conferred but from the casual connection with the other in an adventure in this country in which self-interest as in the other side of the water stimulates zeal.' Nevertheless Sellar received his commission in 1811 as 'a proper person for Collecting the rents of our Estates in the County of Sutherland; for keeping Accounts of the expenditure thereof, for paying attention to the various rights of the Tenants, to the fulfilment of the conditions of their Tacks . . .'

He had been given responsibilities that would bring him into close personal contact with people, many of whom spoke only Gaelic, a language he never understood. For these people Sellar expressed throughout his life the utmost contempt. 'Their seclusion,' he wrote, 'places them, with relation to the enlightened nations of Europe in a position, not very different from that betwixt the American Colonists and the Aborigines of that Country. The one are the Aborigines of Britain shut out from the general stream of knowledge and cultivation, flowing in upon the Commonwealth of Europe from the remotest fountain of antiquity. The other are the Aborigines of America equally shut out from this stream: both live in turf cabins in common with the brutes.' It remained to be seen whether Sellar had come as a philanthropist among these savages, or (as Falconer had warned) as a greedy adventurer intent on driving them from their lands for his own profit. The Countess was already expressing her own doubts about him in 1811. 'Sellar has no sense and perhaps we may be as well without him,' she wrote. 'Young is the important person, the other is nothing without him.' The Countess showed perception as well as a deep concern, but events were to prove that these could not counterbalance the circumstances of her life. However conscientiously she tried to fulfil her role as a Highland Chieftainess, she was in fact the busy wife of an English nobleman, an absentee with her powers delegated to underlings over whom it was difficult to exercise an adequate control.

The consequences had been grave in the 1770s, more ominous still in the years since 1806. The decade that had now opened was the one in which she and her family were to be branded with an infamous reputation; in which the legend of Sellar was born; and over which modern historians apply such peculiar personal epithets to one another according to their particular points of view.

The wholesale disappearance and suppression of documentary evidence of what took place during the years immediately following the appointment of Young and Sellar have merely served to augment all these phenomena. Bitter memory, verified at scattered points and often derided when it could not be verified, told of the alarming bustle throughout the land, as surveyors went about the task of dividing it into sheep farms; sheep farmers appeared in response to public advertisements of properties that were to be let; wholesale summonses of removal were served upon the inhabitants. Sellar paid his first visit during this period to the jewel of Strathnaver, the strath from which the province took its name, where Loch Naver lay beneath Ben Klibreck and its river flowed north to the Atlantic. Here he decided to carve out the richest sheep farm of all for himself.

Sellar stated later that 'it was the mildew of 1812 that convinced us of the impolicy of keeping a highland population on land fit only for grass', and which spurred the estate managers to remove people from the inland valleys to the coasts so abruptly. A crop failure was bound to affect with particular severity the communities of the Naver valley which had been overcrowded by people evicted in previous removals, and as these were now faced with the prospect of another clearance to make way for Sellar's own sheep farm, their plight had been rendered even worse. For they could have felt no inducement to break in the meagre patches of remaining land among the rocks for cultivation when there was little likelihood of being left to reap any harvest from them. Even the mission station at Achness had been allowed by a pious population to fall into disrepair because it seemed unlikely that it would be needed much longer.

Yet the argument of climate could have had nothing to do with the recommendations that Young had made for the improvement of the English estates of the Marquess of Stafford. These were studied by Stafford's new Commissioner in London almost immediately after his appointment. His name was James Loch, and he was born in the same year as Patrick Sellar; but although he was a Scotsman he had studied English law in London.

Reading the Highland Commissioner's proposals for a rural society of which he knew even less than he did of Sutherland's, Loch remarked with surprise: 'a tenancy of 200 years standing Mr Young did not consider as deserving of attention.'

In the north the Countess had made clear her concern for the welfare of her people, and Young and Sellar fed her with lip-service to the same ideal. But what the inhabitants of Sutherland experienced was something very different. To all their other anxieties was added the harshness with which Sellar went amongst them, extracting the last penny of their rents and arrears, particularly from those who would soon be removed. As he remarked of the 1813 rental, 'I knew that the people would not meet me, but I also knew that if I was not found at my post, it would stand them as a good apology for not paying at all and, in the numerous removals now going on, and so necessary in the proper arrangement of the estate, it needs *much* vigilence to prevent them from carrying with them their last rent.' Once again the Countess showed herself well-informed, despite all the distractions of her life in the south. Writing to her husband from Dunrobin in July 1814 she said: 'the more I see and hear of

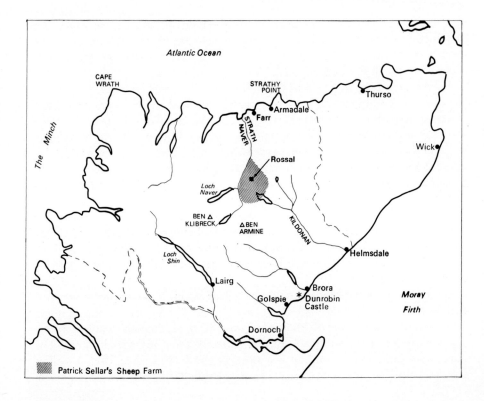

Patrick Sellar's Sheep Farm

Sellar the more I am convinced he is not fit to be trusted further than he is at present. He is so exceedingly greedy and harsh with the people, there are heavy complaints against him from Strathnaver in taking possession of his farm.' Obviously there is a time-lag between these comments and what had been going on in remote valleys.

It was in the strath of Kildonan that the first serious eruption took place. Here the people were given what amounted to six months' notice to begone, so that their lands could be converted into three sheep farms, and the arrangements for their resettlement were once again ridiculous. For they were not invited to move to Helmsdale where their river reached the sea, or along the plains beside the Moray firth where they might have learned the dual occupations of crofter-fishermen – the declared objective of the master-plan. They were ordered to join the communities of the north coast where cultivable land was already scarce amongst its rocky headlands, and where there were no natural harbours from which to take up fishing in the noto-riously dangerous waters of the north Atlantic. Some of the evicted were perhaps not to be resettled at all, according to the estate memorandum of 1806 which proposed that the families of those who had joined 'other regi-ments to the two which the Marquis and Marchioness recommended' should be removed altogether at the general set. The management's policy was to resettle only those of 'good character', however that might be interpreted; and no interpretation was required.

The 'riots' that broke out in Kildonan were described later by the Rev. Donald Sage, son of the local Minister. 'The measures for their ejectment had been taken with such promptness, and were so suddenly and brutally carried out, as to excite a tumult among the people. Young had as his associate in the factorship a man of the name of Sellar, who acted in the subordinate capacity of legal agent and accountant on the estate, and who, by his unprincipled recklessness in conducting the process of ejectment, added fuel to the flame.' Sage recorded that 'the formidible riot, which was reported to have for its object the murder of Young and Sellar, the expulsion of the store-farmers, and the burning of Dunrobin Castle, amounted after all only to this, that a certain number of people had congregated in different places and had given vent to their outraged feelings and sense of oppression in rash and unguarded language. It could not be proved that a single act of violence was committed. Sellar laboured hard to involve my father and mother in the criminality of these proceedings, but he utterly failed. The peasantry, as fine as any in the world, were treated by the owners of the soil as "good for nothing but to be cast out and trodden under feet of men". '

The protest did cause as much alarm as Donald Sage remembered, and prove as harmless. Troops were ordered from Fort George to Dornoch, while a warrant was issued on 27 January 1813 to 'search for seize and

*Dunrobin Castle*

apprehend' a list of ringleaders. Young wrote to James Loch on 7 February, describing the culprits: 'such a set of savages is not to be found in the wilds of America.' He had planned to resettle them where 'the sea would have afforded constant supplies of fish both for the people and for export' while they could have enjoyed excellent crops. Yet they 'rose in a body and chased the valuers off the ground and now threaten the lives of every man who dares to dispossess them'.

Three days later the Sheriff Substitute Robert Mackid held a court at the inn of Golspie attended by the Procurator Fiscal, at which he heard how one of the men named in the warrant 'told the Deponent with tears in his eyes, that he was glad to see him as he wished to communicate a message to Lady Stafford's Manager and the Sheriff, which was that if any man who came down to Golspie upon Wednesday was apprehended as was the case a few days ago at Helmsdale, that there would be such news of it as never happened in Sutherland before, as there would be three hundred men assembled on that occasion'. The meeting in Golspie inn ended dramatically as Mackid recorded. 'The Sheriff Substitute having attended here this day for the purpose of proceeding in the examination of evidence . . . finds it impossible for him to proceed with safety to himself and the other members of Court, in respect the house is now surrounded by a lawless mob assembled for the avowed purpose of preventing judicial investigation. . . . The Sheriff is under the necessity of adjourning to Dunrobin Castle.'

The largest number of any one surname in the warrant were Sutherlands, one of them in the service of the Minister of Kildonan. Since this was part of the ancient territory of the Gunns, it is not surprising that these provided the next largest number, while there was a sprinkling also of such local names as Mackay and Gordon. 'Their orators,' sneered Sellar, 'declared that they were entitled to keep possession of *their* grounds, and would allow no shepherd to come to the country.' On 20 February Young met the leading rioters in person and obtained from them 'a petition to Lord and Lady Stafford begging forgiveness'. By the time the troops arrived in March the people of Kildonan had become 'perfectly submissive' and arrested rioters were released, to Sellar's disgust. 'I saw six of the ringleaders feasted at Rhives parlour, Mr Young drawing ale for them,' he did not forget to mention later. But at least the ungrateful people had been removed to what even James Loch (who had never visited the north coast in his life) was describing by 15 February as 'small but comfortable arable farms on the lea coast of Armadale'.

Not all of them, however, ended their days on those barren, windswept, overcrowded headlands, where the ruins of their long-deserted crofts are still to be seen. A delegation from Kildonan had travelled to London to petition Parliament about their plight, and although their petition was rejected there, they were received by Thomas Douglas, 5th Earl of Selkirk, the outstanding philanthropist of his age amongst the Scottish nobility. Selkirk devoted his entire life and his fortune to promoting a humane and scientific policy of emigation. This Lowlander had already established successful colonies of Hebrideans in Nova Scotia, learning their language in order to be able to converse with them as he accompanied them on their long sea journey, filling his notebooks with details of their difficulties and wants. Now he was planning to provide a much larger mainland home for the Gaels on Red River in Upper Canada, and he enquired whether any of the people of Kildonan would like to emigrate there. Over a thousand men, women and children applied – an impossible number for him to cope with. Selkirk travelled to Sutherland and held conversations with the Countess, who appears (though the evidence is scanty) to have adhered to the opinion she expressed in 1805: 'we foresee in spite of Lord Selkirk that in a few years this country will be benefited by preserving its people to a reasonable degree.' Evidently many of its people now felt otherwise, but Selkirk could do no more than to select over ninety of them, including forty sturdy young men, whose departure from Stromness

*A Crofting township on the north coast of Sutherland*

in Orkney he witnessed on 28 June 1813. They were the most homogeneous group that he had yet been able to assist, and he shared the Rev. Donald Sage's opinion of the people whom Sellar had described with such contempt. 'The Sutherland men,' he wrote, 'seem to be both in person and in moral character a fine race of men.'

It was in 1813, too, that James Loch first visited Sutherland, tearing himself away from the heavy responsibilities to which he had been appointed so recently in order to discover for himself what was going on in the far north. He inspected the admirable developments of the east coast, the roads and bridges and villages that were being planted between its plains and the fishing grounds of the Moray Firth. Young had warned him in February: 'if Lord and Lady Stafford do not put it in my power to quell this banditti we may bid adieu to all improvement.' Troops had been sent: the danger had proved illusory: Loch was able to return reassured, and to inform the Home Secretary Lord Sidmouth that despite the scurrilities of certain London journals all was well in the north.

The management prepared to embark on a more extensive clearance than ever before. At Golspie on 15 December Patrick Sellar outbid all local offers for the Strathnaver sheep farm, with financial aid from the Staffords, and was given entry at Whitsun in 1814, which fell on 26 May. He met the tenants of the Countess on 15 January, selected those whom he would allow to remain on the ground, and promised that new lots would be ready for the remainder (of good character) by 20 April – which would give them five weeks in which to remove. In March Sellar toured the area, serving notices of removal and making sure, as he himself said, that they paid the last penny of their rent before they left. At Whitsun Sellar personally supervised the clearances from his sheep farm although the promised lots on the north coast were not marked out by then, neither had any survey been made to discover whether the grounds proposed for resettlement were capable of supporting life. Many of the lots made available after this hiatus, whose ruins may still be seen, lay in peat bogs or on bare rock. Neither was it any more feasible to fish from here in open boats with oar and sail than from Armadale or Strathy to the east, even if the people had possessed adequate gear or experience in seamanship.

A year later Sellar explained that the object had been for the people to be 'brought down to the coast and placed there in lotts under the size of three arable acres, sufficient for the maintenance of an industrious family, but pinched enough to cause them to turn their attention to fishing'. In those crowded centres of destitution beyond the mouth of the Naver river it was often the women who tried to catch fish off the rocks while their menfolk broke in ground that had never been worked before because it was unfit for agriculture, while they drained bogs, and carried soil on their backs to lay in tiny patches among the rocks. 'The shores of the county,' Sellar continued his attractive picture, 'washed by the Atlantic ocean, near the mouth of the Pentland Firth, abound at all seasons with fish of the first quality.'

Among the communities cleared were those around Loch Naver and in the upper Naver valley which had been overcrowded by people evicted in 1806–8. Young had spoken severely about their treatment when he aspired for the post occupied by Cosmo Falconer. Now he presided over a removal in which those evils were to be repeated on a far larger scale, and in which some of the people involved were experiencing them for the second time.

Of all the townships involved, it was Rossal that witnessed the incidents for which Sellar was brought to trial in 1816. Rossal lies north of Ben Armine, beside the Naver river, in the angle between the roads that run south-east to Kildonan and south-west to Lairg. Today it is preserved as a historic monument, with its ruins of about seventy buildings scattered about within an area of sixty acres enclosed by a stone dyke. The ground is fertile, its plough-rigs still discernible. This may not have been an Arcadia, but its homes possessed doors with metal hinges, and crockery that would have disgraced no peasant household in 1814. Examination has not revealed that any of the buildings within the dyke were destroyed by fire: but then nobody ever asserted that they were.

The incident that led to a charge of culpable homicide against Sellar occurred at a hut outside the dyke, a dwelling typical of those that had created miniature shanty-towns outside such townships since the first clearance of 1806. In it lived a man called William Chisholm, whose evidence at the trial was given through an interpreter, since he spoke no English, and who was described then as a 'tinker' and a 'worthless character'. With him lived his wife and her aged mother Margaret Mackay. It was further stated in court that Chisholm's relationship with his wife was a bigamous one, though no evidence was brought to support any of the allegations against him. The circumstances in which his house was burnt and his mother-in-law died were witnessed by a young stone-mason of Rossal named Donald Macleod, whom Sellar himself cited as a witness before his trial, decades before Macleod published the account of the Sutherland clearances which has excited such lively controversy.

But it took more than a solitary incident, whether fabricated or not, to create the outburst of indignation which erupted in Strathnaver in the summer of 1814.

While Sellar completed the clearance of his sheep farm, his superiors reacted with a curious ambivalence to the fuss that he was causing. It was in July 1814 that the Countess remarked that Sellar was 'exceedingly greedy and harsh with the people', in the same month that she replied to the first petition saying 'that if any person on the estate shall receive any illegal treatment, she will never consider it as hostile to her if they have recourse to legal redress'. Yet she later invited James Loch 'to encourage Sellar in trouncing these people who wish to destroy our system'. For his part, James Loch conceded that the clearances had been 'hurried and improvident' and he recalled Sellar's 'quick sneering biting way of saying things which I do not think has made him popular with anybody'. William Young confessed to Loch that 'the Strathnaver people certainly got too short notice and should have had longer time to move off, I admit it but the fault was none of mine'. He too recognised that 'Sellar has many enemies'.

During 1815 these raised a subscription to meet the cost of prosecuting Sellar, and Robert Mackid travelled to the Naver valley to take evidence. Having done so, the Sheriff Substitute arrested Sellar, imprisoned him in the jail at Dornoch, and wrote a most improper letter to the Marquess of Stafford at the end of May, saying that 'a more numerous catalogue of crimes, perpetrated by an individual, has seldom disgraced any country, or sullied the pages of a precognition in Scotland!!!' Sellar knew how to make enemies, and it was already well known that Mackid was in the front rank of them: but it is difficult to assess the degrees of personal malice and of indignation that moved Mackid to such improprieties of behaviour and language on his return from Strathnaver.

*Sheep Gathering in Sutherland*

Sellar's response to his treatment is a classic example of its type. He now saw himself menaced by 'barbarous hordes'. In vain Loch tried to restrain the extravagance of his language. On 26 October 1815 he wrote to remind him of the advice he had given Sellar when they had met at Dunrobin. 'It was carefully to avoid a certain ironical mode of expression, which does you more mischief than you are aware of. Look back to the copies of all your letters. . . . The same is the case when you speak of the Highlanders both of the better and the lower ranks.' The attitude of Sellar had indeed become that of a naked racist. Now he was developing a persecution complex also. He wrote to Loch in May 1816: 'The consequence I expect from this settlement of this conspiracy is just what succeeded the Kildonan conspiracy of 1812. . . . That is, not a repetition of the *same* attack but an attack of a different nature; unless the family do in their wisdom *mature* such decisive measures as may convince the *people* that it is dangerous for them to engage in such atrocious measures.' A fortnight earlier he had been acquitted in Inverness of the charges brought against him.

During the interval between Sellar's arrest and his trial eleven months later, his employers were careful to avoid even the appearance of influencing the course of justice. 'You will I am sure fully appreciate the delicacy of Lord and Lady Stafford's situation,' wrote Loch in June 1815. 'If they were to communicate any thing which might be construed in favour of Sellar it would be said they were using undue influence in attempting to protect their factor.' At the same time the Countess showed her characteristic concern to discover what had really been going on. In August she invited the Rev. David Mackenzie, Minister of the huge parish which extended the entire length of the Naver valley, to visit her at Dunrobin. 'He says the people in Strathnaver are excellent people if not misled by those to whom they look up. . . . He is ready to contradict the false statements in the papers from his knowledge.'

How could she have failed to feel reassured? 'The result of the conversation and information received from the ministers is, that the Parish of Strathnaver is going on exceedingly well. The people all settled and contented and applying to fishing on the coasts of Sutherland and Caithness; very well disposed.' Not far from the Minister's manse beside Farr Bay the number of tenancies around Naver mouth had increased from 14 to 98 between 1813 and 1815. By 1816 Loch discovered that there were 408 families, numbering some 2,000 people, totally unprovided for, and simply squatting on the estate. In August of that year George Macpherson Grant M.P. reported: 'The lands of Strathnaver are stated to be set in allotments, no vestige, however, of allotment appears.' Once again the Countess had been hoodwinked; this time by the local Minister.

It is sometimes supposed that the Sellar legend grew entirely out of events that occurred before the year 1816, so that it is contradicted by the verdict of his trial. In fact the worst was still to come, and is sufficiently exemplified by Sellar's own statements and actions after his acquittal even if Donald Macleod's *Gloomy Memories* are dismissed as fiction. 'A first point is to make the enemy *pay the expenses of the war*,' he wrote as he set out to hound Robert Mackid the Sheriff Substitute to his ruin. It was, he said, of 'great consequence that our new Sheriff . . . be no "Gael" nor "Mac" – But a plain, honest, industrious *South* country man.' As for all the other Gaels and Macs who surrounded him in Sutherland, 'now is the happy hour to give them battle'.

The Gaelic Chieftainess whom he served had expressed an increasing disapproval of him ever since 1811. Whatever the Rev. David Mackenzie may have said to her in that August of 1815, he had written to Loch in the same month, refusing to contradict 'the circumstances regarding Mr Sellar since they have a foundation, however highly exaggerated'. On 3 October 1816, months after Sellar's acquittal, Loch wrote to the Countess that he possessed 'less discrimination than it is easy to believe, and was really guilty of many very oppressive and cruel acts'.

Why then was he permitted to continue them? On 23 October Loch confessed: 'I regret as much as you do that Sellar was continued as he has been. It was (I fairly own it) my fault and I must be answerable for the consequences. But I was applied to, to do it by Macpherson Grant, just as I was going away and I spoke to Lady Stafford without sufficient reflection. I have however told everybody that it is only a temporary measure. It is all Sellar deserves at Lord and Lady Stafford's hand for much injury done them in disposing the minds of the people against all reasonable change.' Loch added that he would perform any service for the Staffords except to 'embark my character in the same vessel as him'. In this letter to William Mackenzie from Richmond, Loch reveals that what concerned him was the reputation of the Staffords and his own, rather than the misfortunes of Sellar's victims.

On examining the administrative documents of Young and Sellar's five years' management, Loch discovered that the credit of his employers had suffered in another respect. Young had poured out Lord Stafford's money like water, and large sums had disappeared without any receipts to account for them. Although rents had trebled between 1803 and 1815, expenditure had increased nine times, so that an estate which had formerly yielded a large income was now an encumbrance. 'You have no idea,' Loch told an uncle, 'either of the inaccuracy and unsteadiness of execution, the total want of plan, the lavish expenditure, or the total disregard to the people's feelings which characterised the whole management.' In one sphere, however, there was no want of plan, and that was in Sellar's preparations to enlarge his enormous sheep farm without delay. After he had at last been removed from his factorship in July 1817, the Countess wrote to Loch in October, warning him against giving Sellar the slightest legal loophole to evict people summarily and without humane provision for their resettlement. 'We must not give him any promise of entry,' she insisted, 'unless sure of being able to keep it.' She was discovering new definitions of his character. 'Sellar is so strict a lawyer,' she said now, and a year later, 'Sellar is too sly and refining upon his plans by concealing half.'

By the time the Countess wrote that in November 1818, Loch had rejected the warning which the Rev. David Mackenzie sent him in February. Only the less fertile side of the Naver river had been cleared in 1814, and now it was proposed to evict the inhabitants of the opposite bank also. The coast, Mackenzie declared at last, was rocky and infertile besides being 'already thoroughly inhabited'. The ocean was dangerous, the people ignorant of seamanship and without boats. Loch replied, ordering Mackenzie to tell his parishioners that they must make the best of it. If the accounts of Donald Macleod, of the Rev. Donald Sage and of the witnesses questioned by the Napier Commission are dismissed as apocryphal, the history of what followed must wait until the editor of the Dunrobin papers finds the time to release more evidence. But so far as the legend is concerned it sufficed to ensure that the innocent as well as the guilty were swept into the general anathema pronounced to this day throughout the world. The person who probably deserved it least was the shy, bookish man who had married a Highland chieftainess, and allowed his fortune to be spent in Sutherland as she desired. For the last six months of his life he enjoyed the newly created title of Duke of Sutherland, and never was distinction more dearly bought.

> My curses on the Cheviot sheep.
> Where are the offspring of the excellent people
> I said farewell to when I was young,
> When the Mackay country was made a desert?
>
> Loch my lad, you got death:
> If you got justice, you got heat.
> The devil should have lost his left hand
> If he didn't give you a welcome.
>
> Duchess of Sutherland, are you at rest?
> What has become of your silken gowns?
> Have they protected you from corruption and the worms
> That are eating their way into your coffin?
>
> First Duke of Sutherland, filled with deceit,
> Filled with prejudice in favour of the Lowlander,
> Had I been taken prisoner by the Jews
> I would rather have taken the hand of Judas.
>
> Despicable Sellar, you are in the grave.
> If you got the reward you deserved
> The fire which you set to the thatch
> Is even now crackling at your beard.[4]

It is one of the most curious aspects of this story that these Gaelic verses are not more extravagant than some of the 'history' with which they have had to contend. For James Loch compromised the integrity of an extremely conscientious character by attempting to whitewash the Sutherland management in a published *Account of the Improvements* which is at variance with what has survived of his privately expressed judgements. Whatever the Countess did or did not know, the evidence of her information is sufficient to involve her in a similar charge of attempting to safeguard her personal reputation by promoting an account which she knew to be false in significant particulars. Even the editor of the Dunrobin manuscripts has described Loch's *Account* as a wholly false picture, while Dr Eric Richards has called it a 'somewhat despairing defence'.

But it was seized upon, as it was intended to be, as the authentic account of what had occurred up to 1820, and especially by Patrick Sellar's family. It is

*opposite page, Sellar as an old man*

significant that this systematic and highly disciplined man should not have married until 1819 when he was nearly forty years old. He raised a large family and among his descendants were several who achieved outstanding distinction. And it is a not uncommon paradox that his family held him in an esteem as high as the detestation which he excited in so many people beyond their circle.

One of Patrick Sellar's sons published a defence of his late father's career in 1883, in which he was able to quote from James Loch's *Account* that 'of the people removed from Kildonan it is related merely that they were settled near the thriving village of Helmsdale, with the exception of some who preferred going into Caithness'. No mention of those attractive arable farms on the headland of Armadale. As to the second clearance of the Naver valley against which the Minister of Farr protested, Sellar's son was able to say: 'Mr Loch relates, in 1820, that the mass of the removed tenants were then settled on the coast, and were adopting with alacrity the cultivation of their land and the prosecution of the herring fishing.' How Sellar secured an entry in the august pages of the Dictionary of National Biography might baffle any investigator, but there one of his grandsons was able to commemorate his career in Sutherland as a rescue operation. 'In consequence of the periodical failure of the crops in the straths and river valleys, the crofters were removed to settlements on the coast.'

So it has continued up to the present. Sellar's son wrote in 1883 that his father retained his factorship until November 1818, and that the second clearance of the Naver valley did not take place 'till after Mr Sellar ceased to be factor'. The truth of this is confirmed by Dr Eric Richards, though with the additional information that 'Sellar was grudgingly given temporary control until July 1817 when Francis Suther took over the management'. That is the very month in which the Countess wrote to Loch, warning him to give Sellar no legal loophole that would enable him to evict people at over-short notice.

The cool-headed Dr Gaskell has, however, adopted a different interpretation of this important matter of the relative timing of Sellar's resignation from the factorship under pressure, and the second Strathnaver clearance. 'He continued to clear farms in Sutherland for his employers until 1819, and then retired from their service to devote himself to sheep-farming at (sic) Strathnaver.' Being untrue, this statement casts a most unfair aspersion both on the Countess and on James Loch, comparable to some of those found more excuseably in the legends.

In fact, ever since Patrick Sellar walked free from the court-room at Inverness in 1816, people have had to decide whether it is the legends he inspired that contain the more history, or the histories of his career that contain more legends.

## Gaelic originals of quotations

Pages 40–41

Tha Sellar an Cuil-mhàillidh
Air fhàgail mar mhadadh-allaidh
A'glacadh is a'sàradh
Gach aon ni a thig 'na charaibh.

Is truagh nach robh thu'm prìosan
Ré bhliadhnan air uisg is aran
Is cearcall cruaidh de dh'iarunn
Mu d'shliasaid gu làidir daingeann.

Shellair, tha thu nis 'nad 'uaigh,
Gaoir nam banntrach 'na do chluais.
Am milleadh rinn thu air an t-sluagh,
Roimh 'n àm seo fhuair thu d'leòr dheth.[1]

Page 44

Bha mi coimeas nan àrmunn
Ri deadh àmhainn bha feumail
An déidh a teine a bhàthadh
'S gun bhi làthair ach eibhleag.
Ach tha mi fathast an earbsadh
Am beagan aimsir an déidh seo
Gum bi an t-sradag ud Beataidh
'N a teine lasarach aoibhinn.[2]

Pages 45

. . . Tha mi faicinn faileas
De nithe bh'ann bho chéin,
Nuair bha pobull Israeil
'San Eiphit ann am péin.
Thug e le làmh làidir iad
A mach bho Pharaoh féin,
A's dh'fhosgail e an cuan doibh
Nuair luathaich e 'nan déigh.

Tha mi faicinn deuchainnean
An tràthsa air gach làimh,
Teaghlaichean bha urramach
Air leagadh mhàn an ceann,
Seirbhisich 'nan Uachdarain
Is oighreachan 'nan clann,
An talamh làn de dh'éiginn –
A Dhé, có sheasas ann?[3]

Pages 62

Mo mhollachd aig na caoraich mhór'.
Càit bheil clann nan daoine còir
Dhealaich rium nuair bha mi òg,
Man robh Dùthaich 'c Aoidh 'na fàsach?

Loch mo chridhe, fhuair thu bàs:
Ma fhuair thu ceartas, fhuair thu blàths.
Gun caill an Donas an làmh cheàrr
Mur bi e càirdeil còir riut.

Bhan-Diùc Chataibh, bheil thu'd 'shith?
Càit bheil nis do ghùntan sìod'?
Do chaomhainn iad thu bho'n fhoill 's bho'n fhrid
Tha 'g itheamh measg nan clàraibh?

Ciad Diùc Chataibh, le chuid foill,
'S le chuid càirdeas do na Goill,
Gum b'ann an Iutharn 'n robh a thoill
'S gum b'fheàrr leam Iùdas làmh rium.

Shellair shalaich tha 'san ùir.
Ma fhuair thu'n gràs ris 'n robh do dhùil
'N teine leis do chuir thu'n tùthadh
Tha fuaim aig nis ri t'fheusag.[4]

# The Glasgow Cotton Spinners

## Hamish Fraser

On 22 July 1837 John Smith, a cotton spinner, was out shopping with his wife in Clyde Street, Glasgow, at the traditional working-class shopping time of between 11 p.m. and midnight on Saturday night (when food was cheapest), when he was shot in the back. Before he died in the Royal Infirmary three days later Smith told the Sheriff-Substitute of threats he had had from spinners. Smith, an Irishman, had continued to work as a spinner during the strike of the Glasgow cotton spinners that had been going on since April. In the parlance of the time he was a 'nob'. A group of employers offered a reward of £500 for information leading to the conviction of the perpetrators of the crime, and the Crown offered a further £100 together with a free pardon to anyone, not the actual perpetrator, who provided information. Two informants approached Sheriff Alison and, on the basis of their story, Alison, accompanied by Captain Miller, the police superintendent, and a force of police, entered the 'Black Boy' public house in the Gallowgate, where the committee of the cotton spinners' association regularly met, and arrested those present. Most were eventually released but the officers of the spinners' association, Thomas Hunter, the president, Peter Hacket, the treasurer, Richard McNeil, the secretary and James Gibb, the assistant secretary were brought to trial together with a William McLean, who was believed to have been employed actually to commit the murder. The trial and the particularly severe sentences imposed by the court were to cause a major setback to the development of early Scottish trade unionism, deterring many workers from joining unions in the following decades.

'The place was full of women, young, all of them, some large with child, and obliged to stand 12 hours each day . . . the heat was excessive in some of the rooms, the stink pestiferous, and in all an atmosphere of cotton flue.'

*Cotton Spinners on trial, 1838*

That was the sight that 'froze the blood' of the Radical M.P. John Arthur Roebuck – a man not notably squeamish – when he visited a Glasgow cotton mill in 1837. The horror of the conditions under which the factory operatives laboured was confirmed time and again by observers. Temperatures of 80° to 100°F were common and everywhere was the noise and fine dust from the cotton thread. Few spinners survived much beyond the age of forty in such conditions.

The spinner was the key worker in the mill, operating a spinning mule and there were about a thousand spinners in Glasgow mills in the 1830s. Earnings varied depending on the quality of thread being produced, but an experienced fine-thread spinner could expect to earn as much as 40s. a week, a rate of earnings as high as any skilled craftsman could hope for. Out of this, however, he had to pay the wages of his helpers, or piecers as they were called. These were in many cases his own children and their task largely consisted of crawling under the machines to fix broken threads and keeping the machine free from dust. A piecer would probably have entered the mill at the age of nine and would work an eight hour day, six days a week, for 2s. 6d., always assuming that the Factory Act of 1833 restricting the hours of children in mills was obeyed, and in the Glasgow of 1837 that was a doubtful assumption. By the age of seventeen a male piecer could expect to be earning perhaps 6s. 3d. and hope to become a spinner. 'To get his own wheels' was the piecer's ambition, but this depended on wheels becoming vacant at the right time due to the death or departure of a spinner, and a number of the piecers were men in their twenties who were always ready to take over from the regular spinner when he was off.

Carding, roving and finishing processes generally took place in the same establishment and about three thousand workers were employed in such processes. In addition, there was a similar number of carters, porters, warehousemen and general labourers, usually casually employed, but dependent for their livelihood on the mills. The bulk of weaving at this time was still carried on by handloom weavers working at home or in small workshops. There were about 18,000 handlooms in Glasgow and its suburbs and a further 13,000 in surrounding towns working for Glasgow manufacturers. The powerloom had been coming in gradually from the beginning of the century, but was still suitable only for the weaving of coarser fabrics. The application of steam power to weaving had pushed the industry into factories, but, in the majority of cases, these were apart from the spinning mills

*Factory scene in 1840*

and there were only about 15,000 powerlooms in Glasgow in the mid-1830s.

The cotton industry had come to Scotland at the end of the 1770s with a mill at Penicuik in Midlothian and another at Rothesay on Bute. Scotland had a number of attractions for the aspiring cotton manufacturer. There was a well-established linen industry and, therefore, an experienced labour force; there were ample supplies of water and these were essential for powering the machines of the new industry; and there were good communications with America, the supplier of raw cotton.

Because of the need for water-power the early mills were frequently situated in quite isolated places. To attract workers to such mills the employers provided housing for whole families, and operated in many cases an exemplary paternalist system usually accompanied by a strict factory discipline. Whole new communities appeared, totally dependent on the cotton mill: Dale and Owen's New Lanark is a good example.

The improvements in James Watt's steam engine freed cotton spinning from the shackles imposed by water power and mills began to be opened in the towns. Glasgow had particular advantages of cheap fuel, good transport, and a large and dynamic merchant community. In addition, employers in Glasgow could draw on an ever-growing pool of labour. Partly cause, partly effect of this had been the transformation of Glasgow from 'one of the cleanest most beautiful and best built cities in Britain' of Daniel Defoe's day to a dirty, already over-crowded city of nearly a quarter of a million in the 1830s many packed into made-down houses of the eighteenth century or into the already notorious closes of the central city. Between the two censuses of 1821 and 1841 the population of Glasgow increased by more than 75 per cent.

The growth of the cotton industry in the city was rapid, with 39 mills in 1796 and over 100 thirty years later, and this from a total of under two hundred Scottish mills. Renfrewshire had some important mills at Paisley, Linwood, Johnstone and elsewhere, but Lanarkshire and particularly Glasgow dominated. The mills tended to be clustered in Calton, where firms such as James Dunlop and Co. and John Dennistoun and Co. had their mills; in Anderston, where there stood the great six-storey edifice of Henry Houldsworth & Co in Cheapside Street with its workers' tenements, 'Houldsworth's barracks' next door, and William Graham and Co's Lancefield Mill; and in Bridgeton the mills of Bogle and Ferguson and of McDougall and McPhail among many others.

Not that there was a great deal of enthusiasm for factory labour among the native population or, indeed, among many of the immigrants. The factory was strange, dangerous and unpleasant. To enter it was to lose one's independence, for it meant the imposition of the discipline of time: the factory bell; and the discipline of the overseer: the belt for the young, the fine for the adult. Many of the new immigrants to the city had been forcibly displaced

*Black Boy Close*

from the Highlands, but, as was frequently remarked, the Highlander took to factory discipline as a deer to the plough. In contrast, the Irish, coming across on a 4d. fare from Dublin or Belfast in increasing numbers from the 1790s onwards, seem to have shown aptitude and enthusiasm for factory work that was much commended by employers. Unlike what seems to have been the situation in Lancashire, Irish immigrants quickly found their way into the spinning jobs and made up a considerable proportion of the skilled labour force.

The teeming thousands crowded into the wynds and closes within sound of the factory bell. There, in overcrowded rooms and cellars or in the most primitive of common lodging houses, they faced misery and disease. The diseases of the urban environment, typhus, typoid, smallpox and, once in a generation, the terrifying cholera, took their terrible toll. In the second half of the 1830s death rates in the city rose to over 32 per thousand, a figure that hid the two or three times higher mortality of the closes off the High Street. Well over 2,000 perished in the typhus epidemic that hit the city in the summer of 1837 and, in some parts, the disease was probably endemic.

For many, drink gave the only succour from misery. Lacking the inconveniences of licensing hours, one tenth of Glasgow's houses were places for selling drink: 2,200 public houses and spirit shops. Beer and ale were available, but the relatively new whisky which the Irish and the Highlanders had popularised was what was drunk, and anything else was, as the Sheriff of Lanark declared, 'a mere provocative to the whisky'. Drunkenness was commonplace even at work. Partly this was a hangover from a more traditional society and partly it was a product of resentment at the disciplines and the misery of the new industrial society. Birth, marriage, completion of apprenticeship, a new job, a new man coming to work, any excuse to break with the tedium of factory life produced what rapidly became drunken celebrations and there seems little doubt that the amount of alcohol consumed contributed to the violence which was so much a part of early nineteenth-century Glasgow.

Compared with many of their fellow workers, the cotton spinners were among the better off. It was probably a desire to maintain this position that brought about trade-union organisation among the spinners soon after 1800. Despite the laws against 'combinations or conspiracies' (the two words were regarded as synonymous) of workers, trade unions continued to exist, in many cases under the guise of friendly societies. A Society of Lanarkshire Operative Cotton Spinners was recognised as a friendly society by the local Justices of the Peace in 1810. It is clear, however, that the main concern of the society was not to collect money for widows, orphans and sick members, but to keep up wages and to try to limit the number of those who could enter the trade of spinning. Attracted by the high earnings, increasing numbers were making their way into the Glasgow mills and with labour readily available wages would fall. The union's concern was to keep 'incomers' out of the Glasgow mills.

In 1810 the master cotton spinners formally associated for the first time in an attempt to break the powers of the spinners' society, which was reputedly trying to insist that only union members be employed. The associated employers proscribed the Friendly Society of Operative Cotton Spinners and required their employees to sign a document dissociating themselves from the society. It is doubtful whether this action succeeded totally in breaking the spinners' union and there were still sporadic strikes at individual mills from time to time, but adverse trade conditions were not conducive to trade-union advance. In 1816, however, the union was reorganised into the Association of Operative Cotton Spinners which steadily began to build up strength.

The fundamental aim of the new Association was the traditional one of keeping outsiders away from the Glasgow mills. In the years after 1815 the spinners had before them, in the plight of the handloom weavers, a telling example of what could happen to wages in a trade in which there was no restriction of entry. The once-prosperous weavers found their earnings plummetting to 15s., 10s., 8s. and even less, as more and more immigrants, landless labourers and demobbed soldiers turned to weaving as a way of earning a living. The spinners were determined that their trade would not suffer the same fate. According to the rules of the Association members were bound—

to refrain from instructing any individual in the art of spinning, except such as are sons or brothers of a spinner, who may have been, or is at present a member of this association; and it must be remembered that such persons can only be admissable by having served their time as piecers.

In addition there was an entry fee of £1.

That they were not altogether successful in restricting entry is evident from the recurring cases of violence towards newcomers and the continuing concern of the spinners' association with the problem of surplus labour. The building of the Broomward factory by James Dunlop and Co. in 1819, specifically with the intention of employing women in the formerly male preserve of spinning, highlighted the constant threat to the male spinners' position and there were assaults on the women workers as well as an unsuccessful attempt to burn down the mill. Nor was the union altogether successful in maintaining 100 per cent union membership. There were plenty who from either lack of resources or lack of inclination were not prepared to go on strike or who were ready to take the jobs of striking workers, and these strike-breaking 'nobs' (as they were usually labelled) were subject to vilification and violence. Throughout the early 1820s there was a number of examples of attacks on strike breakers. In September 1820, one James Cairney had vitriol thrown in his face; in 1823, McKenzie Phillips received the same treatment, reputedly for his refusal to pay a union levy.

Violence and threats of violence were not confined to fellow workers. There were threatening letters to managers like Patrick McNaught of James Crombie's Anderston Mill, where women spinners continued to be employed, and, when reminders of his 'jeopardy and hazardious predicament' failed to move him, the mill was set on fire.

In a highly competitive industry like cotton spinning the union was able to take advantage of disunity and mutual suspicion amongst the employers and many of the cotton masters were willing to concede to the union control over who should be employed, rather than to risk loss of trade. At the same time, however, there were many grounds for complaint by the workers. In April 1823, for example, the sixty-five spinners of Houldsworth's mill in Anderston came out on strike against what they believed to be fraudulent assessment of sizes of yarn; excessive fining for minor misdemeanours; payment in tokens in lieu of cash wages; and the officiousness of overseers who were regarded as 'too vigilant'. On this occasion the employers struck back by reviving their association and instituting a general lock-out, with the result that there was a fairly rapid capitulation by the strikers. Some concessions *were* won, such as the abolition of token payment and modification of fines. The masters, however, reasserted their right to employ whom they would without reference to the union.

A period of high demand for workers as trade boomed in the autumn of 1824, coupled with the repeal of the Combination Laws, encouraged the spinners to seek redress of further grievances. This time the focus of attention was Dunlop's mill where the spinners struck against the imposition of payment from the workers for 'wear and tear' of the machinery and in protest at the inadequate supplies of drinking water provided. They also sought to be allowed to take in what was euphemistically described as 'suitable refreshment' in the afternoons. The main stumbling block to any agreement was, however, the spinners' insistence that one of the overseers be dismissed. In other words, the familiar issue of management's prerogative on who should be employed was raised once again and the employers, as before, responded with a general lock-out. For four months, the spinners' union held out and few broke the united front. The one or two who did faced a threatening mob and half bricks through their windows.

Attempts at compromise met with constant rebuff from the employers' association which seemed determined to destroy the spinners' union. During January 1825 there were signs of a break, with numbers of spinners returning to work, and by the end of the month the strike and lock-out were terminated. Much bitterness remained, particularly because blackleg labour were allowed to retain the jobs they had obtained during the strike, and there was some harassing of the new workers. There is some evidence that most of the harassment was a product of youthful exuberance rather than of systematic intimidation. Most of those brought to trial for violence against 'nobs' were young piecers. One serious incident was the shooting of John Graham, which was followed by riots in Calton that required the military to disperse them. Eventually, an unemployed spinner, John Kean, despite being defended by the able Edinburgh advocate, Henry Cockburn, was found guilty of attempted murder and sentenced to a whipping in front of the gaol-house, followed by transportation for life to Botany Bay. In a confession, Kean implicated the union in the violence, an implication indignantly denied by the spinners' union. Employers and others, who were keen to get the laws against combinations of workmen restored, tended to assume official union involvement in the violence, but little hard evidence of such involvement was ever produced. What the union does seem to have done, however, was to buy out some of the new workers by paying to keep them out of work until they could get employment at the regular rate.

The depression in trade in 1826 and 1827 brought redundancies and short-time working for many spinners and there were a number of nasty incidents. One John Walker was transported for life in 1827 after pleading guilty to the charge of shooting at a non-union spinner. At the same time, however, employers and the union co-operated in getting uniformity of wage rates throughout the district. As a result, the industry entered a decade of relative industrial peace. Because of technological improvements that increased the spinners productivity, earnings rose to 44s. a week and more, leaving the spinner more than 29s. per week clear after he had paid his piecers. The one issue that did sour relations between employers and unions was the support given by the union to the campaign by Michael Sadler, Lord Ashley, Richard Oastler and others for shortening the hours of labour in factories. James McNish and other Glasgow spinners described the pale and emaciated children who worked in the hot, dust-filled Glasgow mills for twelve hours a day, while Kirkman Finlay voiced the employers' view when he announced,

I am yet to learn of any proof or colour like to proof that shows the employment of persons in well-conducted factories for twelve hours in the day is unfavourable to health.

Judging from the evidence presented to the Select Committee of 1831, the *Morning Chronicle* commented: 'It appears that the most barbarous of the Yorkshiremen are outdone in barbarity by the Scots.'

The spring of 1836 brought an 'extraordinary and unprecedented prosperity' to the Glasgow cotton industry and the employers fulfilled the promise made nearly a decade before that when things improved a rise would be given. With little pressure the spinners obtained a rise in rates of about sixteen per cent. Within months, however, prices were beginning to fall and the cotton masters found themselves under pressure. Their competitive position *vis-à-vis* Lancashire had never been particularly good and, over the previous decade, had become progressively worse. In Lancashire there had been major technological innovations with new and enlarged spinning 'mules' of as many as a thousand spindles. In contrast, there were few 'mules' in Glasgow of more than 350 spindles. The cost of innovation in Lancashire had been a decade of bitter industrial conflict. The short-term reward for lack of innovation in Glasgow was a decade of industrial peace: the price was a loss of competitiveness.

Signs of crisis in the industry were already apparent when the spinners' union became involved in a strike against William Dunn, one of the largest of Scottish textile manufacturers. Most of Dunn's mills were outside the Glasgow area and he had not conformed to the uniform wage agreements that had been gradually evolved in the years after 1827. On a number of occasions in the 1830s the union had dissuaded Dunn's employees from pressing for higher wages, but, in October 1836, 102 spinners at Dunn's Duntocher mill struck work and the union gave them backing. The change of policy on the part of the union can only be adequately explained as a response to pressure from the Glasgow employers who objected to the 'unfair' competition from Dunn. Faced with a threat that their own wages would be cut, the Glasgow spinners backed the Duntocher men. From the start the strike was a mistake. To no avail the union expended more than £3,000 in the sixteen week strike. As one of their number summed it up, 'We lost our money, created dissension among the members and the wages remained at the old price.'

Taking advantage of the financially weak position in which the union now found itself, the Glasgow employers in April 1837 proposed to withdraw the advance of wages given in the spring. Within days, the spinners' association called a strike to resist the reduction. Negotiations came to nothing, as the employers threatened even further reductions and proposed to introduce larger machines. This latter proposal raised the perennial fear of the spinners of a surplus of labour. Less labour was required for big machines and too many workers for too few jobs always tended to push down wages. In May, after the strike had been going on for about three weeks, a number of mills were re-opened using blackleg labour. The re-opening of Johnston and Galbraith's Oakbank mill required a few hundred police and special constables to protect the strikebreakers and a troop of horse to disperse the crowd. In some other mills, the new workers slept in the mill for fear of the crowds that surrounded them. After a fracas at the Mile-End Spinning mill in

Calton, one of the crowd, Keddie, was arrested and brought before Archibald Alison, the sheriff of Lanarkshire. This brought the first intervention in the affair by Andrew Gemmill, a solicitor who acted as legal adviser to many of the Glasgow trade unions. Gemmill persuaded Alison to postpone sentencing Keddie in return for an agreement by the spinners' union to call off the pickets from Mile End.

By July, the position of the striking workers was serious. There was a steady seepage back to work; new workers from outside Glasgow were coming into the mills in increasing numbers; and the funds of the union were so reduced that a mere 9d. or 1s. a week was all that was available to support the strikers. Trade, generally, was depressed, so there was little chance of temporary employment in other jobs. Some spinners were actually begging in towns around Glasgow. Disease was rampant. Appeals for aid in Manchester, Belfast, Greenock and elsewhere brought some return, but by no means enough. Most striking spinners were dependent on family aid, credit from local retailers and the occasional cash or oatmeal hand-out from the union.

The deterioration in conditions inevitably encouraged the wilder elements among the strikers. At the end of May, an incendiary device set fire to the yarn room of William Hussey & Son's mill in Bridgeton and there were rumours, which in fact proved unfounded, of impending widespread incendiarism. In June, Alexander Arthur, manager of the Adelphi mill in Hutchestown received a threatening letter denouncing him as the 'low tool or cringing sycophant of a greedy Tyranical (sic) Capitalist'. In the following month, a burning cannister was thrown through the window of the house of a Bridgeton employer and there were one or two incidents of guns being fired off at the houses of strike-breakers. Six men sought in connection with these incidents absconded.

Suddenly, a new dimension was reached when, on 22 July 1837, John Smith, an Irish strike-breaker employed by Henry Houldsworth and living in the Houldsworth 'barracks' in Cheapside Street, was shot. So far as Sheriff Alison and the authorities were concerned this was the culmination of a campaign of violence and murder against strike-breakers and employers. The stage was set for a showdown as Alison and the police raided the 'Black Boy' tavern in the Gallowgate and arrested the astonished committee. William McLean was apprehended some days after the others, when he had been traced to a house in Campsie, Stirlingshire.

As with previous cases concerning industrial violence the authorities found it very difficult to gather evidence, though Alison was clearly convinced of the guilt of the spinners. In most unjudicial language (it was 'after dinner') he told a deputation of a Calton magistrate and a minister petitioning for the liberation of two still-imprisoned spinners 'that every man of the prisoners ought to be gibbetted . . . and that they were a set of the most cold-blooded murderers he had ever known in the course of his experience as a counsel or as a judge'. The action against the arrested men could have been brought before the circuit court at Glasgow in September, but the investigation was not complete. The case was transferred to the High Court in Edinburgh and after three adjournments because of disputes about the relevancy of the indictment it was called on 3 January 1838, almost the last possible date before it would have lapsed under Scots law.

The judges in the case were the Lord Justice Clerk, Lord Boyle, Lord Mackenzie, Lord Moncrieff and Lord Cockburn, though the last dropped out halfway through the trial to take up his circuit duties in Glasgow. The senior defence counsels were Patrick Robertson and Duncan McNeill, two of the most distinguished of advocates, while Murray, the Lord Advocate and Rutherford, the Solicitor-General led for the Crown. The thirty-four page indictment contained a long list of charges against the defendants: illegal conspiracy to raise and keep up wages by means of threats, intimidation and molestation of other workers; threatening of employers; setting fire to houses, mills and warehouses; assaulting and murdering workmen; setting guards and pickets on the Oakbank Mill to mob and intimidate non-strikers; taking similar action at Ewing's Mile End Mill; conspiring to set fire to Hussey's mill; conspiring to send threatening letters to Alexander Arthur, manager of the Adelphi Mill and to John Bryson, manager of Mitchell & Norris's mill near Greenhead; conspiring to set fire to James Wood's house; and paying McLean £20 to assassinate Smith.

The main prosecution witnesses were cotton spinners, or former cotton spinners, who had volunteered information to the procurator fiscal in Glasgow after the rewards were announced and the defence counsel immediately challenged these witnesses on the ground that, since they were to be given a reward, their evidence could not be relied on, but this was overruled by the judges. Most of these witnesses had been living together for their own protection in Glasgow and Edinburgh gaols since August 1837 and had, therefore, had ample time in which to collude.

James Moat (or Mowat) and James Murdoch, both of whom had been cotton spinners for twenty years, gave evidence of the existence of secret committees of the association, which had been responsible for intimidation, violence and arson in the 1820s. Moat also claimed that he had attended a meeting in the 'Black Boy' on 14 June 1837 at which a secret committee was appointed with the implication that such a committee would be responsible for instigating violence against property and individuals. Both Moat and Murdoch had grievances against the association – Moat had been a member of the committee but had resigned because his brother was a strike-breaker, Murdoch, on more than one occasion had been refused strike-pay.

A number of strike-breakers gave evidence of assaults by strikers. Thomas Donaghey named a group of cotton spinners – not the defendants – who had burst into his room and attacked him and his landlady while they lay in bed. David Gray and Edward Kean told of being knocked about and kicked by a mob who had surrounded the mill at which they worked, and John Farmer and William Gordon told of being stoned through the Cowcaddens and having to be rescued by the police. James Wood, an employer, gave evidence of a blazing canister being thrown through his parlour window and warehousemen from William Hussey & Sons told of the signs they had found of efforts to set fire to the yarn store.

One of the most specific charges in the indictment was that Richard McNeil had actually written the threatening letter that Alexander Arthur had received. Three engravers gave evidence to support the prosecution's claim. Sheriff Alison described the riots at Oakbank and Mile End and he and Captain Miller described the events leading up to the arrests at the end of July.

*Sheriff Alison*

So far the evidence was largely of some violence against 'nobs' and a few references to union links with violent incidents that had occurred in the 1820s. Nothing had been presented to show the role of the defendants in the murder. Here the central figure was the one defendant who was not an official of the union, William McLean, and the key witness, Robert Christie. Christie had been a spinner and a member of the association, but, since 1835, he had been a spirit dealer in Hospital Street, Hutchisontown and, more recently, in the Gallowgate, though he had closed that one five days after Smith's murder. McLean was a regular drinker at Christie's house and, according to Christie, shortly before Smith's murder he had had a conversation with McLean who told him he was going 'to death Mr Arthur' of the Adelphi Mill. McLean was obviously drunk and was loudly proclaiming that he had in his coat pocket something that would 'do the b—r'. On Christie's persuasion, however, he had gone home.

On the Tuesday following Smith's murder, the two met again when McLean called in for a drink at about 7.30 in the morning. He owed Christie some money, but assured him that it would be paid since he was to receive some money from 'the committee' that very day. By 'the committee' Christie assumed that he meant the secret select committee meeting at the 'Black Boy'. Later that morning McLean returned and, according to Christie, a somewhat unlikely conversation ensued:

MCLEAN: I have made one b——r sleep.
CHRISTIE: Oh William, what is that you are saying?
MCLEAN: I made one sleep. (Turning and pointing to a placard on a wall opposite the spirit shop) Do you see yon?
CHRISTIE: Yes, it is £50 of a reward offered.
MCLEAN: No, by God it is £500.
CHRISTIE: For the love of God, William, make your escape, or you will be apprehended immediately.
MCLEAN: There's nae down on me, they are away after another man to Liverpool.

At different times during that day, McLean enlarged on his exploit and he also claimed to have been responsible for beating up Mr Millar, a spinning master at the Lancefield Mill some years previously. As he got progressively drunker he uttered various wild statements including, 'I wish to God that there were three days of darkness, and I would do the b—rs'. On the following day, McLean announced that he was planning to go to America: 'Let who will go to America, I must go'. When the news of Smith's death came out on that same day, McLean swore an oath to Christie and said, 'Little did they think that I did it'.

If Christie's evidence were true it was pretty damning for McLean and certainly gave some support to the prosecution's claim of involvement by the spinners' committee. But, there is much reason to doubt Christie's veracity. On the same day as he had had his final conversation with McLean, Christie had suddenly gone to London, reputedly to visit an uncle of his wife. He was away for ten days and when he returned he was apprehended by the authorities. Only after being threatened with a charge did Christie provide information. When asked in court why he had not gone to the authorities with his information earlier, he gave as his reason fear of the consequences and fear of breaking the oath of secrecy he had taken when he joined the spinners' association at the end of the 1820s. Christie had personal grievances against the association. He had, he claimed, been promised payment by the association to keep out of spinning, but never got the money.

Possible confirmation of a part of Christie's evidence was given, however, by a shipping agent who identified McLean as one of a number of spinners who in mid-July had enquired about steerage passage to the United States. According to this witness, the spinners' association, over the years, had paid the passage of many spinners and their families, most of whom took fictitious names 'not to let it be known that they were leaving the place, for debt or other causes'.

Yet another prosecution witness, Adam Dickson, an elder and Sunday school teacher in the Relief Church, did little to help the Crown's case: he denied that he had ever heard of a secret select committee. A select committee was merely a meeting of delegates from each mill and was called when some important question was to be decided. Unlike the other witnesses, he denied that he had taken any oath of secrecy when he had joined the association thirteen years before. He did, however, report a conversation with McLean on the Monday after the shooting in which McLean had been obviously enthusiastic about the attack on Smith. When Dickson expressed disapproval, McLean made some retort about his 'methodist face', but he did not give Dickson the impression that he had actually been involved in the shooting.

Other evidence against the association came from some of the books and papers seized at the 'Black Boy'. One small book headed 'Emigration' contained the report of a committee set up in 1836 to consider what was to be done about the perennial problem of too many men coming into the trade. The report contained the statement,

We propose that those called illegal men, nobs excepted, presently occupying wheels in Glasgow, should be offered a union on the same terms as those proposed to the west country spinners – viz., by paying £5 as entry money. . . . If any illegal man now occupying wheels should be refractory, and not agree to those reasonable terms of union No. 60 shall receive £5 for each of them they unshop; also £1 for every stranger which they shall keep from occupying wheels. In both cases, No. 60 will be obliged to prove them by a referee, clearly and satisfactorily to the trade, before they receive any money.

By 'No. 60' was meant idle spinners who were members of the union but did not have permanent employment.

A minute book dealing with the attempts of the committee to raise money during the 1837 strike had the entry,

June 15, 1837. – Moved at the general meeting by William Johnstone, and unanimously carried, the names of every nob at present working, and the districts they last wrought in, should be enrolled in a book, and at the end of the strike, unless a change in the list takes place, they be printed; but, at all events, the names of all who remain nobs at the termination of the strike shall be printed, and sent to all the spinning districts in Scotland, England, and Ireland, and that they remain nobs for ever; and a persecuting committee be appointed to persecute them to the utmost.

A clear link between the committee of the association and McLean was found contained in a note carried by McLean when he was apprehended. This was a certificate signed by Hunter, Gibb, Hacket and McNeil, dated 11 July 1837:

This is to certify, that William McLean is a clear member of the Glasgow Operative Body of Cotton Spinners. He has always done his duty, and we recommend him to all our friends.

Such certificates were essential to any spinner planning to move to some other part of the country in search of work. The prosecution case, however, was that this particular certificate was exceptional since it was signed by the officers of the association. Normally such certificates were signed by delegates in the mill where the man worked, who could vouch for his reliability and his payment of union dues.

The Crown case ended late on the fourth day with a presentation of the statements made by the defendants to the Sheriff following their arrest. Hunter had admitted to the existence of a guard committee to watch who was going into work in the mills, but he denied that there was any secret select committee. He denied all knowledge of the book on Emigration, of payments to 'unshop nobs' and of any violence against spinning masters or strike-breakers. Gibb admitted that there were plans to harass those spinners who, after building up debts with the association, had pulled out and gone back to work, but he denied the existence of any persecuting committee. On the 'Emigration' book, he claimed that this was merely a plan drawn up but never put into practice. McLean in his statement had admitted to knowing Smith but he had a detailed alibi for the day of the murder. He had not been at Christie's house, but at four other pubs from 10 p.m. until well into Sunday morning. Somewhere in Calton 'his senses forsook him' and he did not regain them until the afternoon of Sunday, when he awoke in his father's house and learned that he had been brought home about seven o'clock in the morning. At a second interrogation, McLean admitted to having been at Christie's shop on the Monday or Tuesday after the murder, but he denied that he had talked of going to America. The reason for his flight to Campsie had been a fear of being apprehended as a result of false information against him. There was the highly suspicious fact that he had shaved off his 'whiskers' a few days before his arrest. Apparently he had been trimming them with a scissors when he 'made a gaw in them' and had no alternative but to shave them all off, though with the intention of growing them again.

The defence called a number of members of the association as their first witnesses. William McGraw denied the existence of any select committee, but admitted to having been a guard at various mills during the strike. The aim of the guards was to see who was going into work, so that their strike pay or 'aliment' could be stopped, and any influx of new workers noted. 'They were to endeavour to persuade, but never to use violence, or give any bad language.' He did accept that he had heard of 'nobs' 'getting a licking' from cotton spinners, but declared that it was always officially disapproved of and that he had never heard of payments for 'unshopping nobs'. Another spinner, Archibald Mackay, claimed that payment to idle spinners, under the heading 'No. 60', had not been given for about three years, and he too denied any knowledge of violence by cotton spinners: 'I have heard of it, but I did not believe it, and I don't believe it'. Mackay tended to overdo his naivety, as in this exchange:

LORD ADVOCATE: When you came to Glasgow did you hear of vitriol being thrown, and persons being punished for it?
WITNESS: I don't remember ever hearing any person talking about throwing vitriol.
LORD ADVOCATE: You said you had heard of vitriol being thrown, you reflected on it, and thought it wrong. I ask you when did you hear of its being thrown?
WITNESS: No person ever spoke to me of vitriol being thrown. I have heard people talking about it, but not to me. They spoke to one another, and I overhead them.
LORD JUSTICE-CLERK: I have to remind you that there is such a thing as prevarication on oath, and that is punishable. Keep that in view.

Angus Campbell, another witness for the defence, boldly tried a similar parry with the Solicitor-General:

SOLICITOR-GENERAL: What is a nob?
WITNESS: There are several. A new hand that goes into a work, on a strike: he is usually denominated a nob. There are other sorts of nobs.
SOLICITOR-GENERAL: What are they?
WITNESS: I have seen a nob on a walking stick.
LORD JUSTICE-CLERK: The Jury will remember that answer.

Campbell denied that there was anything very sinister in the activities of the association. Like Mackay, he claimed that the term 'No. 60' had not been used for two or three years, and that the term 'guards' expenses' listed in the accounts meant no more than payment to new workers who had been persuaded to quit work: payment to them was kept separately from payment to association members.

The wife of a spinner at Houldsworth's, Helen Smith, gave evidence of conversations with a Mrs Mary Macdonald, who had actually witnessed the shooting of John Smith but had since died in the fever epidemic. According to Mrs Smith, it was clear from Mrs Macdonald's description that McLean was not the assassin. She had described the murderer as 'a little stout man' and McLean was well above average height. A number of other witnesses supported McLean's alibi that he had been drinking in Cameron's public house at the time of the murder.

Two incidents illustrate the relatively inefficient manner with which the Crown case was handled. One of the charges was that the letter threatening Alexander Arthur had been sent by McNeil from Glasgow. A sub-postmaster was able to show that the letter had not been posted in Glasgow, but in Neilston, nine miles away. One further witness cast doubt on part of Christie's story. Reevie, a bill sticker, asserted that, firstly, a poster giving details of the reward was not near Christie's shop, as he had claimed and, secondly, that the poster in the Gallowgate had not gone up until after 3 o'clock in the afternoon. According to Christie, the conversation with McLean concerning the reward had taken place at 11 o'clock in the morning. The prosecution tried to argue that the bill had been posted up the day before, 24 June, but, as Robertson showed, this could not have been the case, since the poster referred to the death of Smith which took place on the 25th.

In his summing up, the Lord Advocate accepted the right of workmen to combine to raise wages, but 'any interference with the rights of individuals, to prevent them from employing their labour as they think fit, is illegal', and, if this were tolerated 'it must be fatal to the commerce, industry, and prosperity of any country'. The cotton spinners' association, he claimed, while harmless on the surface, was 'secret and darkly' carrying out 'deeds of violence and atrocity'. He admitted that the prosecution had had difficulty in gathering evidence, but this, he suggested, was due to the unlawful oaths which members of the spinners' society had to take not to reveal the union's secrets.

The Lord Advocate made great play of the evasiveness of the defendants when they were first questioned. Hunter's denials of all knowledge of the organisation of the society did not tie in with the evidence of defence witnesses. On the question of a secret select committee, the Crown's case was totally dependent on the evidence of Moat. The discrepancy between Moat's

*Gallowgate in 1830s*

evidence of the appointment of the secret committee on 14 June and the denials of this by defence witnesses was got over by claiming that there had in fact been two meetings, one open one of delegates and one secret one which appointed a three man committee.

Duncan McNeill was counsel for Hunter, Hacket, McNeil and Gibb and began by pointing out that the charges related to the period April to June 1837 and not to twenty years before. Yet, the bulk of the evidence of the prosecution related to the years 1818 to 1830: 'But here you are asked to infer the guilt of the prisoners, of offences committed in 1837, from the guilt of other persons of offences committed sixteen or seventeen years ago.' He did not question that guards had been placed on mills, that 'nobs' had been assaulted, that threatening letters had been sent, that Thomas Donaghey's dwelling had been invaded, that combustibles were thrown at Hussey's mill and at Wood's house, or that Smith was murdered. But, what he did dispute was that the four he represented had had anything to do with these offences. The evidence for the appointment of a secret committee on 14 June was solely Moat's statement and this he largely discounts, since all other witnesses, including one called for the prosecution, contradicted him. He argued forcibly that there was nothing to link McLean with the members of the committee, no evidence that they did 'hire, engage, instigate, or direct, or procure' McLean to assassinate Smith for the sum of £20, other than the doubtful and uncorroborated statements of Robert Christie. He ended with a splendid peroration to the jury:

Whether any person was so hired or not, is still only a matter of speculation – matter of doubt and mystery, and it is equally a mystery by whom he was hired. But you are not bound to solve mysteries, or to bring light out of darkness; you are not entitled to disregard, but it is no part of your duty to remove, the doubts that meet you at every step of the case. That is the duty of the public prosecutor. If he demands from you a verdict, involving the lives of your fellow-men, it is his duty to do away all mystery, and to place before you a case clear and free from doubt. . . . Has he done that? Is this case clear and free from doubt? Breathes there the man, so confident of his own powers of discernment, as to say so? Are you, then, to seal the doom of these prisoners in the dark, or to accept of suspicion as a substitute for proof? Are you so impatient of blood, that you cannot wait till the truth is revealed, as it must one day be?

To follow the advice of the prosecutor was to consign those men 'to the hands of the executioner'.

That course, if followed, will indeed put an end to their protestations of innocence; it will indeed extinguish their voices for ever; but it cannot extinguish the voice of truth. In the fulness of time, that voice must be heard, and it may one day ring a fearful peal in your ears, if you act rashly now. . . . Providence has interposed between you and the truth of this deed of blood.

At eleven in the evening, McNeill sat down and the court adjourned.

On the seventh day, Wednesday 10 January, Patrick Robertson rose to make his final statement for McLean. He denied that there was any proof of McLean being involved in a conspiracy with the other defendants. The certificate for McLean, signed by them, was a perfectly innocent note to assist his search for a job in England. As for Christie's statement, he treats these with total scorn: 'such ludicrous stories never came from the mouth of any witness'. All Christie's stories are made fun of and his whole evidence painted as totally untrustworthy.

The Lord Justice-Clerk in his summing up seemed to give credence to the evidence of Moat and Murdoch, but he had no doubts that the evidence of the engravers on the handwriting in the threatening letter to Mr Arthur was 'extremely weak'. He recommended that the Jury find the charge against McNeil 'not proved'. But he went on, 'With this single exception, all the acts of violence charged, are proved to have been committed; and I think most of them are distinctly proved to have emanated from the Association'. On the charge of murder, the crucial question was whether Christie was a perjured witness. This was the question for the jury to decide: 'and in doing so, you will consider the extreme incredibility of a systematic invention, by a person determined to give corrupt evidence, of such circumstances as those which Christie details'. However, he did not think that there was sufficient proof that Hunter, Hacket, McNeil and Gibb had 'hired, procured, or instigated McLean' to commit the murder.

The jury was out for five hours and returned a unanimous verdict of guilty on four of the charges and a majority verdict by eight to seven of not proven on the other eight charges. The defendants were found guilty of conspiring to use 'intimidation, molestation and threats' against non-strikers, of picketing Oakbank mill and Mile-End mill and of hiring people to invade the house of Thomas Donaghey. One difficulty was that this last charge involved acceptance of the existence of a secret committee and yet this had been specifically found not proven. McNeill's objection to this was over-ruled because the jury had been discharged, but McNeill persisted and, after considerable legal debate, the judges accepted that the verdict on the Donaghey incident had to be ignored.

Lord Mackenzie delivered sentence. While accepting that the most serious charges had not been proven, he believed, nonetheless, that the proven charges were very serious, 'a conspiracy to deprive the employers and the employed of their undoubted rights, by force and violence, to rob the one class of their right to employ labourers at such prices as the latter were willing to receive, and to rob the other class of their right to dispose of their labour, at such prices as might be agreeable to themselves'. He admitted that the defendants were 'not otherwise disreputable persons' but had been respectable, but his sentence was seven years' transportation on all five spinners. Lord Moncrieff concurred and the Lord Justice-Clerk denounced the association as 'most illegal and dangerous' and the evidence of its activities had been 'sufficient to appal the stoutest heart'. The association, he asserted, placed workers 'under a species of slavery, which was worse than the worst which had been proved to exist in civilized society; placing them in a condition of subserviency ready to perpetrate the worst crimes at the bidding of their ringleaders, hardened in their hearts, and set against all orders of the community, and under the pretext of promoting the interests of the operative cotton-spinners, bringing destruction on that manufacture in which they were particularly engaged. It is the bounden duty of this Court, to convince the people of this country, that the practice of this most dangerous system will no longer be permitted to exist within the bounds of this kingdom.'

It was almost midnight when the five spinners were taken off to the Tolbooth. The trial had lasted eight days, with the court assembling on most days, including Saturday at ten in the morning and sitting until usually around eleven o'clock at night. The Lord Justice-Clerk's summing up alone had taken fourteen hours: a fact that caused Lord Cockburn to comment that 'a jury may fairly think that the guilt can't be clear which it takes a judge fourteen hours to unfold'.

Reports on the court proceedings had been forbidden during the course of the trial, but after the verdict many columns were devoted to the evidence. Editorial comment was fairly predictable. The *Glasgow Herald* talked of a conspiracy of 'a grossly illegal and tyrannical description', a system of 'atrocious iniquity'. The *Glasgow Courier* believed that the evidence would leave 'a stain upon the national character so deep that a century of repentance will scarce suffice' and the *Scottish Guardian* felt 'bound to state that the apparent disproportion between the magnitudes of the crimes and the leniency of the sentence had filled the minds of all classes in the city with one universal feeling of astonishment if not dissatisfaction'. Only the Chartist weekly, *The Liberator*, edited by Dr John Taylor, took up the men's cause without reservation. In this it reflected the widespread discontent at the whole proceedings among other unionists. A Glasgow Trades' Committee organised petitions and financial support. After the trial, 6,000 copies of a report of the evidence were published by this committee and mass meetings of protest at the sentences were held.

The man who had brought matters to the test, Sheriff Alison, never doubted the guilt of the union. In a speech at the end of the circuit court in January 1838 he declared, 'I rejoice to think that its misdeeds . . . are at length brought to light; and that despite all the efforts of intimidation, and all the attempts at concealment, the acts of assassination and fire-raising, by which terror has so long been spread through the West of Scotland, have been traced to their real source, and the system by which they were perpetrated fully developed.' Two months after the end of the trial he published an article in *Blackwood's Edinburgh Magazine* on the 'Practical Working of Trades' Unions' in which he assumed that the spinners' association had been completely involved in all the crimes charged and seemed to imply that inevitably all trade unions would become conspiracies 'exceeding in the tyranny which they exercise, and the widespread misery which they produce, any thing that could have been attempted by the Czar Peter or Sultan Mahmoud in the plenitude of their power'. Lord Cockburn too had no doubt that the defendants ought to have been found guilty of all the charges. He blamed the jury, and he and others hinted that the members might have been intimidated by the fact that one of the jurymen kept a public house 'where one of the trades or political unions used to meet'. Before the trial in Edinburgh ended Cockburn in Glasgow was meting out seven years' transportation to Thomas Riddle, the one spinner apprehended for the threats to Thomas Donaghey.

As with the radical trials of the 1790s the severity of the Scottish judges shocked moderate opinion south of the border and brought demands for modification of the Scottish legal system. Such offences as those of which the spinners had been convicted would have brought sentences of perhaps three months' hard labour in England. (The case of the Tolpuddle Martyrs was completely exceptional.) A radical espouser of good causes, Thomas Wakley, in the House of Commons, and that most colourful of former Lord Chancellors, Lord Brougham, in the House of Lords, attacked both the legal system and the actual handling of the trial. In a passage of arms with the Prime Minister, Lord Melbourne, Brougham attacked the delays in bringing the men to trial, the mishandling of the indictments and the iniquity of the sentences. Melbourne would have none of this and suggested that the most useful service Brougham could do the nation was to persist in his lectures on political economy to the working classes in the hope that this might lead them away from their misguided unionism, while the ever-reactionary Duke of Wellington called for 'measures to put down this system of combination throughout the country'.

In February 1838 a Select Committee of the House of Commons was appointed to investigate 'Combinations of Workmen'. It concentrated largely on Glasgow and Dublin, and employers and trade unionists from Glasgow gave evidence, as did Sheriff Alison and Andrew Gemmill. The issues of the cotton spinners' case were once again battled over. Gemmill launched an attack on the administration of justice in Glasgow under Alison's guidance, accusing both Alison and the magistrates of bias against workers. He cited examples of former 'nobs' molesting unionists and getting off with a mere 5s. fine for offences not dissimilar to those that had brought seven years' transportation to unionists. He gave an example of Alison sentencing a spinner to three months in the Bridewell for merely using the phrase 'a d——d nob'. Gemmill complained bitterly of what he regarded as a breach of trust by Alison in using against the spinners the arrangement he had worked out with Alison after the fracas at the Mile End Mill in May 1837 to have the guards called off in return for the release of Keddie. He continued to assert the innocence of the four officials of the union claiming, for instance, that if they had felt there was anything in their records to hide they would have done this before they were arrested, since they had been expecting to be apprehended for some days before Alison appeared at the 'Black Boy' and it was on Gemmill's advice that they had not approached the sheriff. Alison recounted the views that he had already published. His attempt to link the spinners' association with two further notorious assault cases, those of Mary McShaffery who had been blinded by vitriol and of Robert Miller a mill manager who had been attacked, came unstuck when Gemmill arranged for a sworn affidavit from Mary McShaffery to the effect that she had never been a 'nob' and had no idea who her assailant had been and from Miller who denied that he had ever spoken to Alison on the subject of his assault and pointed out that there had been no trade dispute when the attack took place. In the end no report was issued and only the evidence was published, evidence that was, thanks to the careful questioning of witnesses by Thomas Wakley, surprisingly favourable to trade unionism.

While the world debated their case the five spinners rotted in the prison hulks at Woolwich where they had been removed a few days after the trial. There they remained until 1840 when the campaign by Brougham and others bore fruit and they were pardoned. Ironically, it was their accusers who ended up in Australia. Moat, Christie and their families sailed to Sidney in August 1838, passage paid, cash to start a new life, outstanding rent and rates all paid by the authorities, as well as a share of the reward money. Murdoch and some of the other key prosecution witnesses sailed for Quebec, suitably compensated.

The spinners' association was not entirely broken by the case. The arrest of the leaders had ended the strike, but many of the strikers failed to get their jobs back and there were occasional outbreaks of trouble against the new hands. In addition the association had contracted substantial debts during the strike, as a result of obtaining meal and other essentials on credit. Something like a thousand pounds was owed to various retailers. Meanwhile members were drifting away from what might be a dangerous and certainly was going to be an expensive organisation. In the end it was technology that destroyed it. Self-actor spinning mules were rapidly brought in at the end of the 1830s and 1840s and these could be worked by young lads and women and spinners of little skill. A remnant of the hand mule spinners' association survived till 1887, however, when the last hand mules were replaced by self actors in one of the Calton mills.

Time has not 'shed its illuminating influence over this dark transaction' as the defence counsel Patrick Robertson believed it would. The truth of the rôle of the spinners' association in Smith's murder still remains obscure. Some time after the trial, in May 1838, James Todd, an umbrella maker, who had been the person who had first brought Robert Christie to the attention of the procurator fiscal as a possible witness, made a declaration that Robert Christie had more or less admitted to him, two days after the murder, that he had been an accessory and that Smith was a 'damned blackguard' who 'had taken indecent liberties and attempted to ravish the young girls who had been employed in the factories as piecers'. Yet another story that went the rounds was that Christie had confessed to being one of four concerned in the murder of Smith along with McLean and to have been responsible for setting fire to Wood's house and for planning to murder Alexander Arthur. The prospect of being arrested caused him to pin the blame on McLean and the association. Certainly, Alison came round to believing that whatever the truth of the matter Christie had been deeply implicated. Finally, another two crown witnesses who had spent some time with Christie awaiting the trial told of a supposed Christie confession in which he had admitted to being involved in the murder together with McLean, a spinner called Brown and a mechanic called Osborne. And the reason? Brown was having an affair with Mrs Smith! Applying Ockham's razor, perhaps the truth was a simple matter of the eternal triangle.

# Madeleine Smith

## Henry Blyth

*'Gentlemen of the jury. The charge against the prisoner is murder, and the punishment of murder is death.'*

These were the first words of John Inglis, the Dean of Faculty, when he opened his speech for the defence in the High Court of Justiciary in Edinburgh on 8 July 1857, in one of the most sensational trials in the history of British jurisprudence.

These were still the days of capital punishment – and still the days of hanging in public, although this gruesome and horrible spectacle was then due to be abolished within the decade.

Thus the prisoner, Madeleine Smith, who was young and beautiful, could expect to be dangling on the end of a rope before a jeering mob within a few short weeks of the jury's verdict if they should find her guilty. And certainly the general opinion throughout Scotland, and indeed throughout Europe, was that she had indeed murdered her French lover by giving him arsenic, and that she deserved the most brutal sentence that the law could inflict upon her.

There were three possible verdicts which this jury of fifteen Scotsmen could return – Guilty, Not Guilty or Not Proven – and there have been many people since that day, both legal authorities and ordinary citizens, who have asked themselves the question 'What verdict would I have returned had I been sitting in that jury's box, and had heard the evidence that was given at Madeleine's trial?'

But one thing at least was certain at this trial. It would be conducted with scrupulous fairness and in the highest traditions of the Scottish Bar, and that the jury would give as honest and as true an opinion as was within their power. The experts would air their views, the witnesses would be questioned, and cross-questioned, and the counsel for the prosecution and the defence would each have their say, but it would be the jury, and the jury alone, who would decide Madeleine's fate in the end. And this they were to be told before they finally retired to consider their verdict, when the Judge, the Right Honourable John Hope, would say to them –

'*You* are the best judges, not only in point of law, but in point of fact. And you may be perfectly confident that, if you return a verdict satisfactory to yourselves against the prisoner, you need not fear any consequences from any future, or imagined, or fancied discovery, which may take place. You have done your duty under your oaths, under God, and to your country, and may feel satisfied that remorse you never can have.'

And no doubt, at the back of his mind, the Right Honourable John Hope was conscious of the fact that this would be a trial which would be discussed for many years to come; and the verdict of the jury would be argued over by countless legal experts, forensic experts and by ordinary laymen.

Yet in fact neither experts nor laymen have *all* the evidence, because the jury at Madeleine's trial must have been influenced by her deportment and behaviour in the dock. They were able to study her for nine days whilst she sat mute and almost expressionless, for at this time a prisoner could not elect to enter the witness box and give evidence under oath.

Thus Madeleine said nothing during the whole of her trial, and it was left to her defence counsel, the Dean of Faculty, John Inglis, to build up his case for her acquittal on the serenity of her demeanour, the innocence in her face and the impeccable standards of her background, for she came of a devout and god-fearing household, and her father was a well-to-do and highly respected member of the Glasgow community.

What John Inglis set out to do was say to the jury, by direct statement or implication 'Can you believe this sweet young girl could be guilty of such a crime as murder?' The jury at her trial were thus able to look at her and ask themselves the same question. 'Can we believe it?'

The modern reader cannot do this. Only one picture of Madeleine is in existence, and this does not tell us very much. The face we see in it is youthful and resolute, but was the air of simplicity and honesty which she contrived at her trial only a mask? Or was she, as some experts believe today, a girl of split personality, who had two very different sides to her character, and was, in fact, a psychopath, and even a little mad?

This we can never know for certain. And even the jury, who watched her so intently for the nine days of the trial, may well have been no more the wiser when they retired to discuss their verdict. It requires a deep insight into human nature for such a mask to be penetrated, and the average juryman, like the average reader, may well lack this insight.

One clue at least has been forthcoming in recent research into her case. A hand-writing expert, who is accustomed to assessing character in order to help the police, has examined Madeleine's hand-writing in great detail, and his findings are of interest. When he made his examination, he was not told whose handwriting this was, or anything other than that it was the writing of a young woman.

'Is there evidence of a split personality?' was one of the questions put to him. And he replied –

'Yes, there is a definite split personality in this case. She can be ruthless and act the part of a romantic.'

'What is the character of this woman?' was another question. And the reply to this was –

'She is hard-headed and pitiless. No sensitivity. No principle when she wants anything.'

But a juryman, if he could have been presented with such evidence, might well have preferred to judge the prisoner's character on his own experience of human nature, and the behaviour of the girl in the dock. He might then have convinced himself that this was not a just assessment of her, and that she was, indeed, an honest and god-fearing young woman who could not have been capable of the crime with which she was being charged.

The key to the trial therefore lies in Madeleine's character; and, to a lesser extent, in that of her alleged victim, the young Frenchman, Emile L'Angelier, who became her lover and whom she permitted to seduce her in the woods outside her father's country house, Rowaleyn, at Rhu.

One thing is undeniable. Madeleine was the product of a typical, respectable mid-Victorian, upper middle-class Scottish background. There was nothing about her parentage or her home life to suggest that she might grow up to become a murderess.

But there was also nothing about her parentage to suggest that she might grow up to become a sensual and immoral young woman who found the sexual act exhilarating, and gloried in this exhilaration. Indeed it was almost inconceivable in the Victorian era that any well-bred and devout young woman could feel such emotions stirring within her, for the whole purpose of the Victorian upbringing was to deny and suppress all such sensual emotions.

Evidence of Madeleine's sensuality was abundantly forthcoming at her trial, where her many passionate and uninhibited letters were read out in open court; and Madeleine's prospect of acquittal was therefore further jeopardised by the traditional Victorian assumption that immorality and criminality must be inextricably linked. The Victorians assumed that a chaste young woman would be free of sin, and that an unchaste one could be guilty of almost any crime. But this argument has no foundation in truth.

Madeleine Smith was born on 29 March 1835, at West Regent Street, in the centre of Glasgow. Her father, James Smith, was a prominent architect in the city who enjoyed the friendship of many wealthy and influential people. He was, in many ways, a typical Victorian, straight-laced, high principled and a devout churchgoer; and the master in his own house.

*The Smith family (Madeleine, age 16, is the tall girl next to her father)*

His wife, Elizabeth, who came of rather better stock than her husband, was a timid and negative little creature, very much under the thumb of her husband, whom she looked upon with awe and reverence. They had five children, of whom Madeleine was the eldest, followed by a brother, Jack, a sister, Bessie, a further daughter, Janet, and a final son, James. Madeleine and Jack grew up to be great friends; but Bessie, who was something of a flirt, grew up to be jealous of Madeline, who was far more attractive than herself. The two young ones, Janet and James, were of little account, although Janet was to play an important part in Madeleine's secret love affair with Emile.

In theory, James Smith ruled his household with an absolute authority, dutifully supported by his timid wife, but in fact he was so busy with his ambitious schemes as an architect, and with his determination to acquire wealth and standing in the city, that he did not pay as much attention to his children's upbringing as he might have done.

Madeleine he was immensely proud of, because she was alert, intelligent and a great help to her mother in the running of the house and the supervision of the younger children. But this is not to say that Madeleine and her father never quarrelled. In fact, it soon dawned on Mr Smith that his eldest daughter had a better brain than he had himself, and that she thought more decisively than he did. She tended to argue with him, and questioned his authority, and she was not easily subdued. But his well-to-do friends were much impressed by her, and assured him that he should be very proud of her, as indeed he was.

In looks Madeleine was striking rather than beautiful. As a young girl she had tended to be thin and gawky, with rather too long and pointed a nose and a sallow complexion, but as she grew into maidenhood her face took on an unmistakable allure, her bust filled out to satisfying proportions, her splendid grey eyes assumed a challenging appraisal of the men whom she encountered, and the sallow complexion gave way to a clear-skinned and fascinating pallor. Her hair was jet black, her carriage superb, and her self-assurance considerable.

Madeleine, even in her teens, did not just enter a drawing-room – she commanded it; and it was not long before the men in it were crowding round her.

She was vain, of course, and she loved male adoration. Indeed there was deep in her the urge to dominate the men who were attracted to her. And finally there was in her a half-hidden sensuality which men of the world recognised immediately.

Madeleine's mother was of negative personality, but there was nothing negative about Madeleine Smith. Her strength of character was unmistakable – and formidable.

Yet, contrariwise as such women so often are, it often suited Madeleine to play the part of the simple innocent – almost of the blushing rose. She first subjugated herself before men and then overwhelmed them.

Mr Smith looked upon his eldest daughter with some bewilderment – but of one thing he could at least be assured. He would experience no difficulty in finding Madeleine a husband once she reached marriageable age. She would be able to take her choice – or rather *he* would be able to take *his* choice, for like a true Victorian father he had no intention of letting her throw herself away on some penniless nobody. And on this point he felt that he could rely on Madeleine's own common sense and worldliness.

Even when she was in her early teens he had already earmarked one highly eligible suitor – his own close friend, William Minnoch, who was quite a bit older than his attractive daughter, but was otherwise an ideal future husband for her in every way.

These things he discussed with his negative wife, who said 'Yes, dear' to all his suggestions. She was not only a little afraid of her husband – she was also a little afraid of Madeleine.

In 1851 Madeleine was sent south to London to be 'finished' at Miss Gorton's genteel school for young ladies at Clapton. She returned two years later, when she was eighteen, more worldly and without her Scottish accent, and rejoined the Smith family circle. Mrs Smith was not strong, and now Madeleine took over the running of the house. She had a few years before the inevitable proposal from one of her many admirers would meet with the approval of her father and she would marry and settle down in a home of her own.

Mr Smith was at this time living in India Street, but he was already planning to move into more spacious accommodation in a more fashionable part of Glasgow. His plans for his daughter's future were ambitious, and he now gave her all the money she wanted, and encouraged her to attend balls, concerts and dinner parties.

She was in a position to be selective, and she knew it. Madeleine was a Scot, and like her father she was anxious to make a good marriage. She knew that her father had his friend, William Minnoch in mind for her, and although he was more than twice her age, he yet had much to recommend him, for he was charming and presentable, as well as being very rich. So she fluttered her eyes at him and then looked down and blushed demurely. And William Minnoch, who was not really a woman's man, found his heart beating faster, for she really was an enchanting girl.

It was at this moment in her life that Madeleine Smith fell suddenly in love with a penniless Frenchman.

Emile L'Angelier, whom she probably first met in a book-shop in Sauchiehall Street, was a type of man whom she had never previously encountered, not even in London. There was a deep distrust of all Frenchmen in mid-Victorian Britain. Napoleon III was now Emperor of France, and not only was he known to be a man of dissipated and immoral habits, but Paris itself had by now become an infamous centre of promiscuity and sexual extravagance, where courtesans unashamedly displayed their charms in the Bois, and the leaders of the Government as openly flaunted their mistresses in public. To the Victorians, it was the playground of the Devil.

The average mid-Victorian Briton looked upon every Frenchman as one dedicated to the seduction and defloration of young girls, and therefore to be shunned at all costs.

This was another problem which the jury in Madeleine's trial had to resolve. Was this an accurate assessment of Frenchmen? Was Emile L'Angelier just another French adventurer and rogue, who seduced Madeleine and then finally blackmailed her, or was he a simple and quite harmless young man who became passionately attracted to her and may in fact have loved her far more than she ever loved him?

*Emile L'Angelier*

Emile was in his grave when the trial began, and was therefore a silent witness, but the jury were given many descriptions of him. He certainly looked like a typical French seducer, with his long and twirling moustaches and flamboyant dress, and he certainly behaved like one, with his gallant speeches, his eccentric ways, his uninhibited compliments, and his disgusting French habit – to a Victorian – of kissing a girl's hand soon after he had met her for the first time. It was known that several innocent young Scots girls of the lower orders had already succumbed to his charms, and had allowed him to kiss with passion other parts of their bodies besides their hands. Even so, was he really a buccaneer and a blackmailer?

Did he seduce Madeleine or did Madeleine seduce him? It was a very difficult problem for a simple juryman to decide.

The love affair between Madeleine and Emile, which began at the beginning of the February of 1855 and lasted until his death by poisoning on 23 March 1857, was certainly an uninhibited affair. Both parties wrote long letters to each other, but whereas Madeleine told her lover to destroy all her letters, he in fact kept most of hers, while she burnt nearly all of his.

Why did he keep them? Because they were warm and passionate love letters and he was deeply in love with her? Or because they were wildly indiscreet love letters which he could use to blackmail her in the future? In short, was he an ordinary young man who was in love, or was he just a typical Frenchman whose only aims were to conquer, to deflower, to humiliate and finally to threaten?

There was certainly no doubt that it was Madeleine who made the running after only a few weeks of their meeting. Their correspondence began when he sent her a single rose on St Valentine's Day – 14 February 1855. By late summer of that year she was already addressing him as 'Beloved Emile' and ending 'Adieu, dearest love, and a fond embrace', and signing herself by her pet name, Mimi, or Mini.

On 3 December 1855, she began her letter 'My own darling husband' and ended it 'Much love kisses tender long embraces kisses love. I am thy own thy ever fond thy own dear loving wife thy Mimi L'Angelier'. And in this letter she referred quite unashamedly to the pleasure she experienced when being 'fondeled' by him.

She therefore made no secret of the fact that she considered herself to be in love with him, and believed that he was deeply in love with her; and that she welcomed his amorous advances.

By January of the new year he was visiting her in secret late at night at the Smith home in India Street, and they had already made plans for marrying in the autumn. Yet at this time he was working as a packing clerk with the firm of Huggins and Company, merchants and warehousemen of Bothwell Street, and was only earning the humble wage of ten shillings a week.

Did he genuinely believe that he could support a wife on this modest salary? Or was he trying to ensnare the daughter of a rich man? Was he a romantic fool or a calculating seducer?

One point that must be made about Emile L'Angelier at this stage – and it is a point which must have influenced the jury at the trial – was the state of his health. Emile, for all his Gallic bravado and swaggering demeanour, was a man who was sadly lacking in self-confidence and was a martyr to his nerves, with all the physical ailments that accompany such neurotic disturbances. He suffered greatly from indigestion, and like so many people who are inflicted in this way he consistently ate too much and too fast. He therefore suffered from dyspepsia, diarrhoea, stomach pains and insomnia.

But Emile had other problems, which were in part the result of his generally neurotic state of mind. He also suffered acutely from melancholia and had suicidal tendencies, which were usually brought on when he felt that he was being crossed in love. His basic lack of self-confidence, especially in so far as women were concerned (despite his flamboyancy when in their presence), convinced him that women could not be trusted, and that he was doomed to be betrayed by them.

Finally, he had a record as a child of having suffered from 'falling sickness' – or minor attacks of epilepsy.

He had therefore become a hypochondriac, who was for ever going into chemist shops and dosing himself with various kinds of quack medicines, many of which aggravated his complaints rather than cured them. He also frequently resorted to large doses of laudanum (a tincture of opium), which today would be considered a dangerous drug.

One quack remedy which he relied upon more than any other was arsenic. Arsenic, at this period, was generally believed to have excellent medicinal qualities if taken in small doses. All over Europe males were swallowing it to improve their health and stamina – and to increase virility.

Emile was not strong, and his virility – as is so common amongst men who are always referring to their sexual prowess – was not all that he could have wished.

But he was not the only person taking arsenic. Madeleine had also started buying it by this time. Arsenic was widely – if secretly – used by young women in Victorian times as a cosmetic, to whiten the hands and to improve the complexion; and young women were also known to take it for the same reason as Emile – because it was thought to promote sexual ardour.

But whereas young men such as Emile were happy to buy arsenic quite openly, young women bought it secretly, and – when visiting a chemist – would say that they needed it for poisoning vermin, and above all rats.

Rats were admittedly very prevalent in the basements of old city houses, and arsenic provided an effective means of exterminating them.

Now the ordinary white arsenic looks rather like sugar, so Victorian chemists, in order to prevent it ever being mistaken for sugar, and also perhaps to discourage young people from tasting it, had by law to mix it with colouring matter – usually soot or indigo.

It is – or it should be – one of the fundamental rules for biographers, and all those engaged in social research, that they should firstly examine carefully the medical history of the people whom they are describing. A sick man will seldom behave normally; and it is doubtful if Napoleon would ever have lost the battle of Waterloo had he not been suffering from serious stomach complaints, and was in no condition to lead an army in the field.

The jury at Madeleine's trial had therefore to take into consideration that during this passionate love affair between Emile and Madeleine, both parties were in the habit of taking quack medicines and even poisons in small quantities, though Madeleine far less so than Emile. Emile, indeed, was in a sorry state in every way, his nerves worn to shreds, his self-confidence undermined, and his stomach like 'a druggists' waste-pipe', to quote a phrase used in another famous murder case.

How far did the state of their health affect the outlook and behaviour of these two lovers? Madeleine probably only a little, for she was always a strong and healthy girl. Emile a great deal.

It was inevitable that Mr Smith should, sooner or later, find out about this love affair, for gossip was as rife in Glasgow as in any other community; and it was also inevitable that he should make enquiries about Emile's antecedents, and having found out that he was a penniless nobody, should have forbidden his daughter ever to see him again.

Madeleine dutifully submitted to the paternal ire, promised her father that she would have nothing more to do with Emile – and went on behaving just as before.

It is clear from her correspondence, and from her general behaviour, that Madeleine was a pathological liar. She had no respect whatever for the truth; and her conscience was quite untroubled by this. The fact that she read her bible daily, and that every evening she attended family prayers before going to bed, and bowed her head devoutly when her father intoned The Lord's Prayer, made no difference to her at all. She believed what Byron's mistress, Caroline Lamb, had believed fifty years before – that 'The Truth is what you believe at the moment'. This helped her to tell some monumental lies.

There is no doubt that at this time, during the years of 1855 and 1856, Madeleine had convinced herself that she was deeply in love with Emile and that she wished to become his wife. She repeated this again and again in the stream of passionate letters which now poured from her pen – many of them written late at night after family prayers, and some after Emile had been smuggled into her bedroom with the aid of her personal maid, Christina Haggart, and there allowed to 'fondel' her and commit other intimacies.

The later at night she wrote, the more passionate were her words of love. The writing of long letters was a typical Victorian habit (the Queen herself wrote many pages every day) and now Madeleine abandoned herself to this practice as a means of giving vent to her over-heated imagination.

When spring arrived, the Smith family, as was their custom, took up residence at the country house, Rowaleyn, at Row (now Rhu), on the banks of the Clyde and only a short distance by river steamer from Glasgow; and it was in the woods outside the garden wall that Madeleine finally lost her virginity to Emile. He either deprived her of it, or she willingly offered it to him.

This incident occurred on the night of 6 June 1856, as was revealed by Madeleine in a letter that she wrote to Emile dated 'Wednesday morning, 5 o'clock'. In this letter, which was a very long and exultant one, she showed no remorse over what had happened, and even went so far as to suggest that it might be Emile who was feeling guilty over what had happened; and she told him that he had no need to do so because they were so deeply in love. This letter was signed 'Kindest love, fond embrace, and kisses from thy own true and ever devoted Mimi, Thy faithful wife.'

Thereafter the course of this true love – if it was true love – was by no means smooth. Emile was frustrated, apprehensive and discouraged by the improbability of Madeleine ever becoming his wife. He was also tortured by the knowledge, which she made no effort to hide from him, that his Mimi was also being entertained by other men, and was making herself very agreeable to them.

The real blow fell in the November of 1856, when Mr Smith moved into his new home at 7 Blythswood Square. At first sight this seemed admirably suited to their clandestine meetings, for Madeleine was given a bedroom in the basement, with a window that looked directly onto the street. They could thus whisper together through the bars at night, or Emile could be introduced into her bedroom from the back door by her personal maid, Christina Haggart.

The cause of Emile's distress, however, was that Mr Smith sub-let the top of the house to William Minnoch, who therefore became a member of the Smith household. By now it was clear that he had fallen in love with

*The Smith House in Blythswood Square*

Madeleine, and that she was doing nothing to discourage his shy and tentative advances.

Rumours of all this reached Emile, and caused him the greatest anguish. His rival, as well he knew, was charming and immensely rich. What hope had he now of keeping his hold on Madeleine?

By now Emile had begun to have serious doubts about her trustworthiness towards him; and he was at last beginning to realise that Madeleine was a liar. This was now being brought home to him by the fact that although William Minnoch was paying court to her, and taking her out to the opera and to dinner, she yet continued to assure Emile that she had no interest whatever in William, and that Emile alone was the object of her affections.

By the Christmas of 1856 she was in the habit of talking to Emile through the bars of her bedroom window, which looked out onto Mains Street, and they were exchanging notes. In a letter written to him on Boxing Day she suggested that they should elope, but expressed doubts about how the reading of the Banns could be arranged. By now her letters were unashamedly revealing, and she openly expressed her longing for him to make love to her. Her letter to him on 11 January 1857, and headed 'Saturday night, 12 o'c' (which suggested that it was written in bed) ended as follows –

'A kiss, sweet one, my best beloved, my adored Emile. A kiss to you who fills the place in my heart, you whose image is ever before my eyes, you whose name is on my lips. Adieu, my love, my all, my life, my darling Emile. A kiss, a warm, tender embrace. Adieu. Adieu. Good-night. Bless you, my sweet love. I am thy own ever dear, fond, devoted and ever loving wife, thy own Mimi L'Angelier.'

In another letter, written to him a fortnight later when she was in bed with the candle guttering by her bedside and her sister, Janet, asleep beside her, she spoke of him having but just left her, when she was in her night-dress, and she wrote 'Would to God you had been in the same attire . . . if we could only get married.'

Two days later, on 28 January 1857, William Minnoch proposed to her and she accepted him.

The workings of a woman's mind are often complicated and sometimes inexplicable, especially to the ordinary male; and it is therefore difficult to assess just what Madeleine had in mind at this moment. The evidence suggests that she now decided to take one man but was reluctant to let go of the other.

By now Emile was deeply suspicious, and when, a week later still, she wrote him 'a cool letter' he returned it to her. In reply she roundly upbraided him, told him that their affair was ended and ordered him to return her 'likeness' and all her letters.

He flatly refused to do so.

It was this that finally brought Madeleine to her senses. For the first time in this long affair – and possibly for the first time in her whole life – she lost her head. And she wrote to him in abject distress. 'Emile, for the love you once had for me do nothing till I see you – for God's sake do not bring your once loved Mimi to open shame. . . . Do nothing till I see you, for the love of heaven do nothing. I am mad, I am ill.'

He visited her at midnight on the following evening, and they had a short conversation in Christina Haggart's room.

No one will ever know what happened at that meeting, but it seems probable that she won him over, no doubt by allowing him to make love to her, but he still refused to give her back her letters.

By the following day she was her old self again – writing to him a warm and chatty letter, as if nothing had happened, and signing it 'with kindest and dearest love'. Clearly she was playing for time, and turning over in her mind what action she should now take.

On the next day she sent the house-boy, William Murray, on an errand to the chemist. She wanted some prussic acid. He returned empty-handed, saying that they would not sell him any.

Thereafter, for the next month, she and Emile resumed their old association. He visited her repeatedly in her bedroom, having first been admitted through the back door by Christina Haggart, and Madeleine not only allowed him to make love to her, despite the fact that her sister, Janet, was asleep in the same bed, but also brewed him cocoa to drink.

As this month of February progressed, Emile's health grew steadily worse. He began to complain to his work-mates, and to his middle-aged patroness, Mary Perry, that he was tormented by sudden and violent attacks of nausea, vomiting, diarrhoea and acute stomach pains.

Madeleine also complained of being ill at the same time, and with similar symptoms, but she was never as bad as he was. Nor did these recurrent bouts of sickness prevent her from going on with her arrangements for her marriage to William Minnoch. The date for this was now fixed for 18 June, but she told Emile nothing of these plans, and succeeded in convincing him that she no longer had any affection for William. But it must have been apparent to her that before long an announcement of the forthcoming wedding would have to be made in the Glasgow papers, and the news would then be all over the City.

Emile was still being granted her favours as of old – but he still had not returned her letters. On this point he was proving himself to be surprisingly stubborn.

Now at this time Madeleine became increasingly alarmed by the rats which she declared were to be seen in the cellars at Blythswood Square and also at Rowaleyn. On 21 February she went on a shopping expeditition in Sauchiehall Street, and dropped in to Murdoch Brothers, the chemists, where she bought sixpennyworth of arsenic, mixed with soot, giving as her reason for this purchase 'For Garden and country house'. She had the cost charged up to her father's account.

She saw Emile secretly in the drawing-room at Blythswood Square on the following evening, when she promised to give him a French bible. On his return to his lodgings, he was taken very ill. Madeleine complained of similar ill health.

On 6 March Madeleine was visited by an old friend from her days in London at Miss Gorton's finishing school – a girl named Mary Buchanan from Dumbarton. Mary was to be Madeleine's bridesmaid, and the two girls, greatly excited, set off together on a shopping expedition down Sauchiehall Street to buy clothes for the great occasion. On their way home, and almost as an after-thought, Madeleine entered the shop of John Currie, another well-known chemist, and bought an ounce of arsenic mixed with indigo. The sale was duly entered in the Poison Registry, and the purpose of the purchase given as 'For killing rats'.

The two girls left in the highest spirits, and giggling together at the fact that they scarcely looked the sort of customers who might have been expected to enter the shop to buy a deadly poison!

On 18 March she bought some more arsenic from John Currie – 'for killing rats'.

On the following day Emile went off on a short holiday to near-by Bridge of Allan, without telling Madeleine. He therefore failed to receive an urgent letter from her, begging him to visit her on the night of 21 March. The letter was forwarded on to Emile, who received it on Sunday, 22 March. He immediately hurried home, arriving back at his lodgings at Franklin Place at 7.30 in the evening. He told his landlady, Mrs Jenkins, that he would have to go out shortly on an urgent visit, but he did not say where he was going. Nor did she ask him, feeling no doubt that it was none of her business.

He left the house at nine, and did not return until 2.30 in the morning, when he rang the door-bell violently before collapsing in agony on the doorstep.

Mrs Jenkins helped him up to bed, where he was very sick – a thick vomit, yellow in colour. He continued to suffer terrible stomach pains and frequent bouts of sickness throughout the night.

A doctor attended him at eight the next morning, gave him a sedative and said he would return three hours later, by which time he hoped that his patient might be sleeping.

When he and Mrs Jenkins tip-toed into the bedroom at 11 a.m., it seemed that he was. But when the doctor bent forward to examine Emile, he found that he was dead.

The doctor asked Mrs Jenkins – an intelligent and capable woman – where Emile had been on the previous night, and what he might have eaten or drunk. But she could tell him nothing – only that he had left at 9 p.m. in seemingly good health, and had returned some five and a half hours later in great agony.

The doctor was puzzled by the death, but had no suspicions of foul play, and it was Emile's foreman at work, a man named William Stevenson, who at once began to ask questions. He visited Emile's lodgings, and searched his room. Here he found Madeleine's letter, begging Emile to visit her – and also his diary.

He then insisted on further enquiries being made, and as a result, a post-mortem was carried out. This revealed the presence of a strong irritant poison in Emile's stomach; and it was then that the police began to take an interest in the case, in the person of the Procurator-Fiscal.

On 26 March Emile was buried in the vault of Ramshorn Church, but five days later the body was exhumed on the instructions of the Procurator-Fiscal, and certain organs, and part of the brain, were taken to Dr Penny's laboratory at the Andersonian Institution, where Dr Penny was Professor of Chemistry. As a result of his report, Madeleine was arrested.

The trial of Madeleine Smith on charges of murder and attempted murder opened some three months later before the High Court of Justiciary in Edinburgh – on Tuesday, 30 June 1857. The judge was the Lord Justice-Clerk, the Right Honourable John Hope, assisted by Lord Ivory and Lord Handyside.

The prosecution was in the hands of the Lord Advocate, James Moncreiff, and the defence of Madeleine rested on the shoulders of the Dean of Faculty, John Inglis.

Thus there were assembled in Court on that June morning some of the finest legal brains in the whole of Scotland. These were men of learning and of the highest integrity, so that Madeleine was assured of a fair trial.

The jury, as is the custom in Scotland, consisted of fifteen men, the majority of them of relatively humble background – including a bootmaker, a clerk, a cabinet maker and a cow feeder – but their foreman, or 'Chancellor', William Moffat, was a person of some standing, a teacher. According to Scots law this jury would be required to return one of three possible verdicts – Guilty, Not Guilty or Not Proven.

But the most important point which the modern reader must consider was the fact that in both Scotland and England at this time a prisoner could *not* elect to go into the witness-box and give evidence on his or her behalf. Not until 1898 was the law amended so that a prisoner in a criminal case was granted the questionable privilege of testifying – questionable because many prisoners since that day have elected to go into the box and to submit to

*Scene inside court*

cross-examination, and have done their cause far more harm than good as a result.

Thus Madeleine was required to sit silent through a trial that lasted nine days without speaking a single word in her own defence.

It was generally felt throughout Scotland that the case against her was a strong one.

She had the *means* of killing Emile, because she was known to have bought arsenic on several occasions.

She had the *opportunity* of killing him, because it was known that he had been in the habit of visiting her bedroom secretly at night, where she gave him cocoa to drink – and cocoa was the ideal substance with which to administer arsenic to an unsuspecting victim, because it dissolved so readily in this liquid.

And finally she had the *motive*. Emile possessed a number of her letters, in which she not only repeatedly referred to him as her husband, but also made it clear that she had indulged in sexual intercourse with him, and had greatly enjoyed it.

It has often been suggested that her motive for murder was to silence a man who was blackmailing her with a threat that he would show her letters to her father. But it must have been obvious to a woman of Madeleine's intelligence that murdering her lover would have the very opposite effect – it would almost certainly lead to the publication of the letters. Her motive, therefore, is not to be found in the suppression of her letters but in the invidious position in which she found herself under Scots law at that time. Under the law of Scotland where a man and a woman promise to take one another in marriage at a future date and, after that promise, the woman permitted sexual intercourse the original promise became an accomplished fact. Such forms of irregular marriage were commonplace in Scotland at that time and the average individual was well aware of its implications. These letters could therefore establish that Madeleine was already in fact the wife of Emile L'Angelier, and therefore could not marry her wealthy suitor, William Minnoch. Motive, indeed, for a determined and cunning woman, such as the 'nice Miss Smith'.

The charges of attempted murder, by the administration of arsenic, probably in cocoa, were open to some question, but the charge of murder itself on the night of 22/23 March seemed to be fully supported by the evidence, except on one vital point. Emile had not told his landlady where he was going before he set out that night, nor did he tell her where he had been after he returned in a state of collapse in the early hours of the morning. *And no witness had come forward to testify that he had seen Emile anywhere in the vicinity of Blythswood Square on the night in question.* And Madeleine, in her official Declaration given to the Sheriff-Substitute before the trial, had affirmed that Emile had not visited her on the evening in question, when she had gone to bed early and slept peacefully with her sister, Janet, by her side.

The evidence on this point would therefore have to be circumstantial; but many legal experts believe now, and have believed in the past, that circumstantial evidence can often prove more conclusive than direct evidence. And the circumstantial evidence seemed very strong.

Madeleine was therefore in grave danger of conviction on the charge of murder; and were this to be so she would be hanged in public within a few weeks of her conviction.

The general feeling in both Glasgow and Edinburgh was against her, especially among the women, who considered that her erotic letters were an outrage to common decency. Little wonder therefore that huge crowds assembled outside the Court on each day of the trial, and that reports appeared in newspapers throughout Europe and even in America.

But one man stood between Madeleine Smith and a violent and terrible death at the hands of the public hangman – her defender, John Inglis, the Dean of Faculty. He alone could save her. And it was he who rose on the morning of Wednesday, 8 July, to face this tremendous task and to deliver one of the finest speeches ever given in a British Court of Law, beginning with the words –

*Gentlemen of the jury. The charge against the prisoner is murder, and the punishment of murder is death.*

A distinguished Judge of the High Court today, Mr Justice Thesiger, has said of this speech, 'It was his task to persuade a Scottish jury before a Scottish judge that the deceased, her lover, deserved to be murdered by his client but that it was doubtful whether she was responsible. In both England and Scotland such an argument requires delicate presentation.'

His aim, in short, throughout his speech, which lasted for nearly five hours, was consistently to blacken the character of Emile, to picture him as an unprincipled seducer and a ruthless blackmailer, and as consistently to present his client, the pale and beautiful young girl in the dock, as a person of innocence and chastity who had been most shamefully deceived.

Now this was the period of great advocacy – of pious exhortations to the Almighty, of eyes raised to heaven, of towering eloquence, and of impassioned pleas to the jury. It was a period when the whole drama of a murder trial was exploited to the full, and when a famous advocate's greatest assets were an actor's delivery and a splendid presence.

John Inglis was ideally suited to the task in hand. He had been engaged by Mr Smith regardless of cost in order to save Madeleine, and the choice had been a wise one. John Inglis was a man of transparent honesty and honour – a splendid figure in the prime of life with his slim figure, his unflinching gaze and his soft, persuasive voice. He was a born actor, just as his client, as well he knew, was a born actress. Together they had a part to play – she the lonely and tragic figure in the dock, so beautiful, silent and serene, he the gallant Sir Galahad battling to save her life.

In retrospect now, and considering this trial after a period of over a century, one is tempted to wonder which of the two gave the greater performance during this nine-days trial – the prisoner or her defender.

It was said of Madeleine at the time that she entered the Court like 'a belle entering a ballroom'. And each day the first sight of her brought forth a gasp of admiration from the body of the Court. She looked magnificent.

What was John Inglis's private assessment of her? This we shall never know. He was certainly impressed by her beauty, her composure and her proud defiance in the face of the terrible accusations that were made against her. Yet he was an upright and Godly man, who can only have been shocked by the sensuality of her nature, which her infamous letters had so clearly revealed. In the whole of his long life – and he lived to be over eighty – Madeleine was said to be the only client whom he ever visited in prison before the trial. Normally he was indifferent to the personality of the prisoner whom he was defending, for his only aim was to subject the evidence presented to the Court to such a searching examination that every flaw and weakness in the prosecution's case should stand revealed.

But he was yet a normal man, with a normal man's reactions to a beautiful woman. He was also a man of the highest moral standards. Was he secretly

*John Inglis*

attracted by Madeleine, or was he secretly repelled by her? Or was his attitude towards her a mixture of both?

No one will ever know.

His opponent, the Lord Advocate, James Moncrieff, was content to rely on an undramatic approach for his presentation of the case against Madeleine. He developed his case against her with quiet logic, allowing the facts to speak for themselves. When the question of her character arose, he quoted her letters to prove that she was a young woman without a moral to her name; but he did not imply what so many of his listeners, including the members of the jury, expected him to imply – namely that because she was capable of acts of gross immorality she was also capable of extreme acts of criminality, including murder. He, too, was ready to attack the character of Emile L'Angelier, and in this he certainly strengthened his learned friend's defence.

'It is no part of my case' he said, 'to maintain the character of the unhappy deceased. The facts in this case make it impossible to speak of him in any terms but those of very strong condemnation.'

Thus Emile, the dissected remains of whose body now lay rotting in his grave in a vault in the Ramshorn Church, found few enough at the trial who were ready to speak up for him, though Moncrieff did find himself forced to concede that Emile was yet 'a man moving in a respectable position, bearing a respectable character, liked by all those who came in contact with him, spoken of by three landladies with whom he lodged in the highest possible terms'.

Indeed his last landlady, the sensible and capable Mrs Jenkins, who was one of the first witnesses to be called by the prosecution, spoke of him with affection and compassion.

Although a great deal of time was spent in calling evidence as to Madeleine's purchase of arsenic, and also of the effects which arsenic would have on anyone who had consumed it, the outcome was straightforward enough. Emile had died from a massive dose of the poison – enough to kill a regiment of men. But there was yet one vital point which arose out of the autopsy. The arsenic which Madeleine had bought had been coloured, but no colouring matter was found in the deceased's stomach.

But Dr Penny, the prosecution's leading forensic expert, and Professor of Chemistry at the Andersonian University at Glasgow, made a telling point when he observed that the colouring matter could be removed 'by peculiar and dexterous manipulation'. And all eyes were turned on the prisoner at this point. Was that the face of a young woman so advanced in crime that she would be capable of performing a difficult exercise in chemical distillation?

Later the same searching look was again focussed upon the prisoner when James Moncreiff spoke of the traditional callousness of poisoners, who were so often capable of contemplating the dying agonies of their victims with 'a coolness that could hardly be believed'.

Thus Moncreiff, despite his distaste for his task, had done it well when he concluded his address to the jury with the words –

'And now gentlemen, I leave the case in your hands. I see no outlet for this unhappy prisoner, and if you come to the same result as I have done, there is but one course open to you, and that is to return a verdict of guilty on this charge'.

But although James Moncreiff had presented a strong case against the prisoner, and had martialled the facts with telling force, he had been handicapped in this on one vital issue. Emile had kept a diary – the same diary which William Stevenson had found when he visited Emile's bedroom immediately after his death. Now this diary could indicate whether or not Emile had set out on the fatal evening to visit Madeleine.

But was a dead man's diary admissible evidence? After long and careful consideration, the judges decided that it was not. The person who compiled it was not available for cross-examination and, if it was to be allowed as competent evidence, it would have meant that any person who felt herself maligned by it could find herself seriously prejudiced thereby, as Madeleine certainly would have been. There was sound reason in law and common sense for the Bench excluding the diary.

So the moment came when John Inglis had to rise and set out on the long journey which would take the jury along the tortuous road which he hoped would lead them finally to accept his belief – that his client was incapable of committing the crimes laid against her, and that she should be acquitted of them.

He opened quietly. He described Madeleine as a beautiful young girl in the prime of life, who had become tragically involved in a romantic love affair in which she had willingly given her heart, and then her body, to a common adventurer who had been wholly unworthy of that love. And for a few moments he allowed himself to speak lyrically about this ill-starred romance.

'Gentlemen, there are peculiarities in the present case of so singular a kind – there is such an air of romance and mystery investing it from beginning to end – there is something so touching and exciting in the age, and the sex, and the social position of the accused that I feel almost bowed down and overwhelmed by the magnitude of the task that is imposed on me.'

He then turned to a consideration of the character of the deceased, a romantically-minded man but one who was yet 'depressed and melancholy beyond description. He was a man of mercurial temperament, never to be depended on.'

In short, the speaker argued, he was a potential suicide, and might well have killed himself. He was always threatening suicide; and there was no foundation in the popular belief that those who threatened suicide never carried it out.

He had consumed a vast quantity of arsenic; and there was also no foundation in the popular belief that a would-be suicide would never take so large a dose. In fact, those who committed suicide very frequently took a far greater dose than was necessary in order to kill themselves. And frequently they killed themselves in the most agonising manner. It had also to be remembered that the deceased was a confirmed arsenic-eater, and had been for years.

Madeleine's letters, the contents of which had so shocked the Court when they had been read out, the speaker dismissed quite easily. His client had fallen into the clutches of a sexual degenerate who had dragged her down into these obscene depths by the power of his hold over her. He had forced her to behave in the way she did.

Did she commit this murder? *Could* she have committed it? She who was so young, so innocent and the product of such a devout and God-fearing family?

'Think, gentlemen, how foul and unnatural a murder it is – the murder of one who within a very short space was the object of her love – an unworthy object – an unholy love – but yet while it lasted – was a deep, absorbing, *unselfish*, devoted passion. And the object of that passion she now conceives the purpose of murdering. Will you be content with conjecture – will you be content with suspicion, however repugnant – or will you be so unreasonable as to put it to me in this form, that the man having died of poison, the theory of the prosecutor is the most probable that it offered? Oh, gentlemen, is *that* the manner in which a jury should treat such a case? Is *that* the kind of proof on which you would convict on a capital offence?'

On the question of motive, he was on more factual ground. In what way would it benefit the accused to murder her lover *unless she had first obtained her letters from him*? For once he was dead, she might never be given a chance to have the letters returned to her. To kill him, therefore, would have been madness.

Then he turned to another impressive point in Madeleine's defence. It was suggested by the prosecution that on the night of the murder Emile gained access to her bedroom, where she was asleep and sharing the same bed as her younger sister; that he awoke her, without disturbing her sister, and that she arose and put a kettle on the fire, made him a very large quantity of cocoa (for only a very large quantity would have hidden the taste of the arsenic from him), persuaded him to drink this very large draught, then presumably allowed him to make love to her, and finally ushered him from the room and out of the side door, still without waking her sister, and without disturbing the cook and the maid, Christina Haggart, who slept in adjoining rooms.

And having administered such a lethal dose to him, could she thereafter have slept so soundly that she and her sister had to be awakened in the morning, when both opened their eyes as though nothing had happened on the previous night?

It was almost past belief. And indeed it was!

And finally he came to the strongest point in his case. The prosecution maintained that Emile L'Angelier had visited her bedroom that night, yet they had failed to produce a single witness to prove that he was anywhere in the vicinity. Nor did he tell his landlady where he had been.

Thus there was nothing to connect his nocturnal wanderings on that night with Madeleine Smith. To maintain that he had visited her was conjecture – pure conjecture – and nothing else. Could a young girl be hanged on such an indefinite supposition?

After he had sat down after nearly five hours, utterly exhausted with his tremendous effort, the last word was left with the Judge, the Lord Justice-Clerk, the Right Honourable John Hope, who addressed the jury with simple directness.

Not for him the rhetoric of the Dean of Faculty. Not for him the impassioned plea for the jury to look favourably upon the prisoner, with her serene and untroubled gaze. He had watched her closely throughout the trial, and her beauty had not escaped him; but he was a man of probity and he made no secret of the fact that he looked upon her as a woman sunk deep in moral depravity, some of whose letters were so shocking that he had refused to read them out, for they had contained intimacies such as 'were never previously committed to paper as having passed between a man and a woman'.

There spoke the Calvinist Scot; but he went on to say that whatever the jury might think about Madeleine's shameless relationship with her lover and her purchase of arsenic, one single fact remained, and that was that '*the case for the prosecution may be radically defective in evidence*'.

There spoke the man of probity and the man of justice, whose only concern was that the jury should come to a just decision.

*Scene outside court*

The jury filed out, led by their foreman, William Moffat, and a hush fell upon the Court; and they awaited this verdict which was a matter of life or death.

After twenty-five minutes, the jury returned to announce their verdict – 'Not Proven'. And Madeleine was free.

There was cheering and shouting in the Court, and this was taken up by the huge crowds in the street outside. Men threw their hats in the air, and women wept.

But in the dock, Madeleine remained as serene as ever, though her face was flushed and her hands trembled slightly. She gave a half smile at the three judges on the dais above her, at the fifteen jurymen who faced her, and at the tumult in the Court below. Then she turned and gave a long, quizzical look at her defender, smiled again and finally withdrew from the dock.

But John Inglis ignored her. He sat with his head bowed in his hands – an actor who had given his all. Now that the curtain had fallen he was utterly drained of emotion.

He never set eyes on her again.

In common with so many other alleged murderesses, Madeleine Smith withdrew into relative obscurity after her trial and lived on to a great age, finally dying on 12 April 1928, in New York, at the age of 93. Throughout this long life she always denied that she had killed Emile, although the usual stories were in circulation of her having confessed to one or other of her friends that she did it, and would do it again if the same circumstances ever arose.

She never showed any grief over the death of Emile, although it is said that she was in the habit of paying for Masses to be said for his soul. She expected to marry William Minnoch after her release, and was genuinely surprised when he refused to having anything more to do with her. Thereafter, throughout her life, she held her head high, and ironically it was her family who suffered most deeply from the memory of her trial, whilst she herself was soon able to erase the memory of it from her mind.

# The Tay Bridge Disaster

## John Prebble

The Board of Trade Inquiry into the Tay Bridge Disaster sat for twenty-five non-consecutive days in the Assize Court, Dundee, and at Westminster Hall in London. It examined one hundred and twenty witnesses, most of whom were co-operative, some were defensive or hostile, and one was plainly drunk. Almost twenty thousand questions were asked, and the evidence given ran close to a million words. When the report of the Inquiry was published in July 1880, it undoubtedly caused the premature death of Sir Thomas Bouch, the designer of the bridge. His was the last life to be claimed by his great undertaking. Twenty had been lost in the construction of the bridge, and seventy-five more were taken in the great storm of Sunday, 28 December 1879. That night the High Girders – the thirteen central spans of the bridge – fell into the Tay, carrying with them an engine, five carriages and a brake van of the 5.20 p.m. from Burntisland. To a considerable proportion of Scotland's population this catastrophe was undoubtedly providential judgement upon a profane people. 'If there is one voice louder than others in this terrible event,' said a minister of the Free Church, 'it is that of God, determined to guard his Sabbath with jealous care!'

Throughout Britain the shock of the disaster was indeed great, although in England, at least, there were few who recognised it as a just punishment upon the irreligious practice of Sunday travel. That shock can still send a tremor through the imagination, even where the details are unknown, and cannot be explained by the nature of the calamity alone. If that were so, it would have been long since obscured by catastrophes of greater proportions now forgotten. It is perhaps remembered because of its effect upon the complacency of the time, upon the Victorians' smug confidence in their industrial supremacy, their arrogant pride in having built the longest and greatest bridge in the world. Disasters were common enough in that age of commercial and imperial growth, and those on a colonial battlefield could always be reversed by the punitive victories that followed. But the self-conceit of the nation never recovered from the fall of the Tay Bridge, and from the unnerving revelations of the Inquiry into it.

The bridge had been the triumphant conclusion of a fierce struggle between the warring railway companies of the mid-century. It was the last effort made by the North British, at a moment when its destruction by the Caledonian seemed inevitable. Although the company came late, almost too late, to an acceptance of the need to bridge the Firth of Tay, the arguments in favour of it had long been indisputable. Rail travel from Edinburgh to Dundee in the eighteen-fifties was an experience which, once attempted, was not repeated if the passenger could think of an alternative. Between him and his destination lay two wide firths to be crossed by ferry, and although the whole journey was no more than forty-six miles it took three hours and twelve minutes, more if there were gales on the Tay or the Forth. The best train of the day, ill-heated and trailing two foul-smelling fish-trucks, left Waverley Station at 6.25 a.m. At Granton on the Forth its passengers transferred to a side-wheel ferry and crossed to Burntisland. Thence a second train took them through Fife to Tayport where another steamer carried them across the firth to Broughty Ferry, and there a third and final train delivered them to Dundee. Infinitely preferable to this purgatory was the Caledonian's longer route via the city of Perth.

Thus it did not require the dreaming of Thomas Bouch to see that a rail line running direct from Edinburgh to Dundee, crossing both Forth and Tay by bridge and opening the north-east to goods and passenger traffic, would restore the flagging fortunes of the North British. Born in Cumberland, son of a sea-captain, Bouch had come to Scotland in 1849 at the age of twenty-seven, to be traffic manager and engineer to the Edinburgh and Northern Railway. His imagination and ambition were inspired by the thought of bridging the Tay, and when his company was absorbed by the North British he took his proposal to his new directors. He was told that such a bridge, almost two miles in length, was 'the most insane idea that could ever be propounded'. Even those who were attracted by the suggestion, and could see that it would bring victory in the bitter war with the Caledonian, were appalled by the estimated cost, £200,000. That year the North British had declared a loss of some three thousand pounds against the Caledonian's profit of more than twenty.

Bouch continued to plan and design his Noble Undertaking, assembling figures of stress and strain, of rivets and bolts, bricks and cement, diligently building the smaller bridges and viaducts that gave him, or so it was thought later, the knowledge and experience to throw an iron span across the Tay. The North British Company's need to survive, allied to the cupidity or selfless concern of business interests in Dundee, must eventually impose serious consideration of the proposal, but a considerable body of opinion argued that such a bridge would most certainly collapse, either as a result of engineering fallibility or divine disapproval. Some who believed it structurally possible were even so convinced that it could never give a profitable return to investors. The more lyrical and derisive of its critics were now calling it 'this rainbow bridge'.

*Sir Thomas Bouch*

The war between the North British and the Caledonian had reached its most violent and bitter stage, with company servants brawling in public, rolling-stock sinking into a deplorable condition, rates falling to suicidal figures, and rival spur-lines competing for minimal traffic. North British share-holders who also had stock in the Caledonian watched the depreciation of their investment with impotent horror, and loudly complained that 'our left hand is fighting our right'. Their dismay was understandable. For once in lieu of a dividend it would seem, the Ordinary share-holders of the North British received a tastefully-printed map of the company's network, as if to show them where their money was being lost. At last men of stronger heart, in the company and in the business community of Dundee, accepted the need for the bridge. In October 1864, the public was offered the prospectus of the Tay Bridge and Dundee Union Railway Undertaking, and a month later Parliamentary notice was given of a Bill to provide for the incorporation of the company. The proposed capital was £350,000, more than enough, perhaps, for Thomas Bouch had now reduced his original estimate to £180,000. 'I will stake my professional reputation,' he said, 'that the cost will not exceed this amount.' The rash assurance was characteristic of his euphoric mood. 'It is a very ordinary undertaking, and we have several far more stupendous and greater bridges already constructed.' He did not say where.

Opposition to the Bill was immediate and noisy, and the Caledonian marshalled an offensive to 'blister the back' of its old enemy. The Dundee Harbour Board, made prosperous by high dues, was alarmed by the thought of goods coming into and out of the town by rail, on a bridge which the first plans placed dangerously close to the port area. The rival city of Perth indignantly declared that the structure would block its seaway communications. The Scottish Central and the Scottish North Eastern railways, already threatened by the Caledonian, knew that they would not survive a northern thrust by the claret and cream carriages of the North British. Behind all these protests there was heard the shrill, small voice of the Dundee Rights of Way Association. If there must be a bridge, it said, it should carry a public footpath.

The sustained clamour of opposition was successful, and two Bills for the establishment of the company foundered before Parliament. The scheme seemed lost, until John Stirling of Kippendavie became chairman of the North British in 1866. He was one of the most influential men in railway history, a man of gentility and honesty in an industry that sometimes seemed to be dominated by rogues and charlatans. At the age of fifty-five he took the ailing company in hand and encouraged its frightened directors and share-holders to fight for its survival. 'We have three hundred stations,' he said, 'yet our traffic per mile is £1,058, while the Caledonian, with fewer lines and

fewer stations, is £1,458.' In September 1869, at a meeting in the Council
Room at Dundee, his enthusiasm and persuasive advocacy, his promise of
North British assistance to the extent of 5¼ per cent of the stock, once more
revived the Undertaking.

In the last week of March 1870, another Bill came before Parliament.
Stirling's cunning and skill had neutralised most of its opponents, and the
Caledonian had all but crippled itself in a last and bitterly competitive battle
against the North British. Perth had been bought off by Stirling's promise –
backed by a change in Bouch's designs – that the central spans of the bridge
would be raised above the rest, giving freeway to shipping. The northern
railways had lost their fight with the Caledonian, and their opposition fell
with it. The Harbour Trustees, reacting slowly to a changing climate, were
first charmed and then gently tricked by Stirling. Peering myopically at his
papers as he addressed meeting after meeting, Old Kippendavie inspired the
nation's trust and loosened its purse-strings. The proposal to weave iron and
masonry through two miles of air and water now excited the imagination of a
people who already knew that all that was new in this century of scientific
achievement must be done by Britain. Pride and profit were powerful
stimulants, and when the Bill received the Royal Assent in July all real
opposition to the Undertaking had been overcome. It lingered only in letters
written to the Dundee press by an old man who lived on the Carse of Gowrie,
and who was unimpressed by Parliament's approval. What could it know of
bridges, or engineering, when the masonry of its own newly-erected building
was already crumbling? He died that year, and departed with one last terrible
warning. 'In the case of accident, with a heavy passenger train on the bridge,
the whole of the passengers would be killed. The eels will come to gloat over
in delight the horrible wreck and banquet!'

On Saturday, 22 July 1871, a day of good sunlight and a stiffish breeze,
the minister of Forgan called for the Almighty's blessing when the foundation stone was laid on the south bank of the Tay at Wormit. The small son of
the resident engineer gave the three orthodox taps on the stone, and the
Undertaking was begun. There was a small crowd only at this ceremony,
Bouch among them. Standing at a discreet distance from the gentlemen was
a handful of workmen. It was to be their bridge, whoever designed it and
whoever contracted for it, whoever made a profit from it. They were the men
who would go out on to the river, who would work against the relentless tug
of wind and tide, who would burrow twenty feet and more into the river-bed,
sweat in hot caissons by the light of penny-candles, choke in foul air, die in
sudden accidents, and endure all for eightpence an hour. But they knew it
would be steady work, Bouch had promised them that there would be
employment for three years, and no one could have expected that it would
take more than twice that time to finish the bridge.

Bouch's plans, as they existed in 1871, proposed a latticed girder structure, carrying a single railway line on tall brick piers from bank to bank. There were to be eighty-five spans, the shortest 28 feet in length, the longest 285. At the centre of the bridge, and for the satisfaction of the city of Perth, there would be fourteen raised spans, the High Girders, each of 200 feet. Whereas on the other spans the line would run along the top of the box girders, it would pass *through* them along the High Girders.

From the beginning there were disappointments and frustrations. A general belief that it was impossible to make accurate bids had produced few tenders from contractors. The first that was accepted came from a firm which shortly afterwards withdrew, upon the death of one of its partners. The second went to Charles de Bergue & Company who agreed to build the bridge in three years and for £217,000, by which figure, it might be thought, Thomas Bouch lost the reputation he had so confidently staked. The contractors' manager on the spot was Albert Grothe, a burly man with a passionless face and a generous heart, much given to lecturing about his work and to writing in *Good Words*. The foundation stone at Wormit had not long been laid when he insisted upon the establishment of a Tay Bridge Co-operative Association, 'victuals at a reasonable price', a kitchen, dining-hall, dormitories and a reading-room. Most of the seventy men and boys who began the building came from Fife and Forfar, the others were itinerant labourers from Ireland and England, and the base of their operations was on the south bank, a small and noisy community of workshops, stores and huts, walls of iron, bricks and timber.

By the middle of September the land abutment had been built with huge blocks of stone, quarried at Carmyllie in Angus. Two piers were already completed, and a third was in progress, rectangular columns to support the girders and built wholly of brick. They were each created from two cylinders of wrought iron, carried out on pontoons and sunk to the river-bed where the water was pumped from them. Then began a nightmare of candle-lit danger as the caisson gangs went down into the cylinders. In a space of no more than nine feet in diameter, men and boys dug for twelve hours at a time, with pick, spade and the claws of their hands. As they dug, the cylinder settled about them, through mud and clay until it rested firmly upon the rock-shelf which, according to Thomas Bouch, was there waiting all the way across the river. The cylinder was then lined with brick, narrowing the interior to a diameter of four feet, the only escape for the sweating men at the bottom. The hollow core was finally filled with cement.

With frequent modifications, changes decided upon by Bouch or Grothe, the building continued for two years, and there seemed to be no doubt that it would be completed in the time promised. And then, shortly after the sinking of the tenth pier, it was discovered that the rock-bed of the river did not, as Bouch had assumed, lie eighteen to twenty feet below the mud from bank to bank. The depth was forty feet in many places, in others there was a crust of gravel only, and one sounding went down 150 feet and still did not find rock. Bouch's confidence was unshaken by this startling discovery and he told the North British that the problem could be overcome by creating solid foundations where natural rock should have been. A Dutch engineer, Gerrit Willem Camphuis with no previous experience of bridge-building, drove piles into the mud and clay and constructed the artificial floor upon which the piers might rest, but these could no longer be the imposing brick monoliths that had marched so boldly from the Wormit shore. Now Bouch designed iron piers to rest upon concrete bases, and the modification introduced new problems of stress and strain that could be solved only by changes in the design of the girders. Iron already cast and brought from England was abandoned, and a foundry was opened at Wormit. These changes were too much for the knowledge and abilities of the contractors, their enthusiasm already weakened by the death of Charles de Bergue, and they withdrew from the undertaking. It was three months before the work was taken up by another firm, Hopkins Gilkes & Company of Middlesborough.

Bouch had made other changes. He altered the sequence of the spans, and instead of fourteen High Girders of 200 feet there were now to be thirteen, eleven of 245 feet and two of 227 feet. Each span took four weeks to build, with over 18,000 rivets holding its struts and tie-bars, and the largest weighed 190 tons. They were built on a staging off the Wormit shore, projecting beyond the planking and with clearance below. When a girder was complete, part of the staging was taken away and two barges were positioned beneath the span. At high water it was taken out to the waiting piers and there it was slowly raised by hydraulic jacks and by the sweating labour of eighty men, twenty feet a day until its ends were higher than the top of the piers. It was aligned between them, and as high tide turned, the water fell and the barges dropped, the girder came slowly down until it rested upon the pier-heads.

Delay followed delay, and five years after that modest foundation ceremony eighteen girders were yet to be erected, but the bridge was now a recognisable, a wondrous reality. In the autumn of 1876, two large electric lights, with parabolic reflectors, were introduced to speed night-work, each 'with an illuminating power equal to 1,000 candles, the current generated by two of Gramme's electro-magnetic machines driven by an engine of four horse power'. The people of Dundee were awed by a marvel that would be commonplace to their grandchildren. At week-ends they took the ferry to Newport and the train thence to Wormit, excited by a closer view of the workshops and foundry, thrilled by the acrid scent of hot iron, and deafened by the noise of hammer and steam. There were other, more distinguished visits, deputations of engineers and architects, Members of Parliament, ambassadors, artists, poets and photographers. The sad old Emperor of Brazil was inspired to think of a similar bridge across the mouth of the Amazon. Prince Leopold, Victoria's youngest son, was carried out by wagon along the line already laid atop the finished girders. He told Thomas Bouch, who sat beside him on a crimson cloth, that he admired not only 'the elegance of the structure, but its solid substantiality'. Ulysses Simpson Grant, victorious general of America's Civil War and until recently her eighteenth President, stumped silently along the bridge behind the wagon that carried his wife and other ladies. When he had walked back, and in response to an enquiry about the noble sensations he must be feeling, he said 'It's a very long bridge.'

It was also malevolent and murderous. From the beginning its creation was a struggle between the courage of the workmen and the forces they were attempting to control. For three weeks one gale blew without let, plucking helpless men from the spans. The collapse of three cylinders on the south shore drowned two more in liquid mud. An unexplained explosion, in the caisson below Pier 54, killed six men inside the shaft and blew others into the water. A winter-night storm, blowing up suddenly from gusts of rain, tore two great spans from their jacks. 'For a second or two,' said a survivor, 'the air around me was brilliantly illuminated by the friction of falling iron.' Before the bridge was finished, a score of men had died in these and other accidents. Their deaths were taken philosophically by those who were not called upon to share the risks. 'Life is not lost,' wrote a correspondent to the Dundee press, 'which is spent or sacrificed in the grand enterprises of useful industry.'

And then the bridge was finished. In six years six hundred workmen had built it with 3,700 tons of cast iron, 3,500 tons of malleable iron, 87,000 cubic feet of timber, 15,000 casks of cement, ten million bricks and over two million rivets. It had cost £300,000. Its total length, from signal cabin to cabin at either end, was one mile 1,705 yards. It rested upon 85 piers, the first fourteen of which, stepping out from the south bank, were of brick, the remainder of iron. It was not a straight bridge, not an arm thrust from shore to shore of the firth. From the south it curved to the left for three spans, then to the right, as if uncertain how to make this terrible crossing. For the first three spans, too, it fell slightly in height, ran level for another three, then climbed like a tired wave to Pier 29. There it ran level to Pier 36 where it began to drop. Before it reached the north bank it swung in an arc to the right, down to a new and handsome esplanade, to a new and handsome Tay Bridge Station with its 'extensive lavatory accommodation, hot-water room, three classes of ladies' waiting-rooms, and three refreshment-rooms of different classes'. A railway line now ran from Dundee to Burntisland, and when the Forth was bridged (a project actively engaging Bouch's mind) there would at last be direct communication with Edinburgh. The Great McGonagall burst into bathetic verse.

Beautiful Railway Bridge of the Silvery Tay,
I hope that God will protect all passengers
By night and by day,
And that no accident will befall them while crossing
The Bridge of the Silvery Tay,
For that would be most awful to be seen
Near Dundee and the Magdalen Green.

*The completed bridge from the north*

The first crossing was made on 26 September 1877. The little engine *Lochee* pulled a small train crowded with ladies and gentlemen of distinction, all aboard at the invitation of the North British and the Tay Bridge Undertaking. Ahead of the *Lochee* ran a pilot engine, and on its footplate was Thomas Bouch, soon to be knighted for his services. The crossing took fifteen minutes, a slow journey on a thread of iron above a sun-spangled river crowded with yachts, steamers, ferries, fishing-boats, barges and wherries. When the train entered the High Girders, and was abruptly enclosed by the fret and lattice of iron, the noise of the wheels changed to a roar, and some of the ladies cried out in mock alarm. Their fear became real when there was a sudden crack of wood, the sound of agonised splintering and a beating upon the roofs of the carriages. A brave young gentleman put his head out of a window and cheerfully reported that there was no serious cause for alarm. Some idiot of a workman had left a wooden staging in the path of the train. The incident added zest to the journey and was a spirited talking-point at the ceremonial luncheon which followed.

That winter, and before the bridge could be opened to the public, Major-general Charles Scrope Hutchinson, Board of Trade Inspector, spent three days examining the bridge from end to end, and three weeks considering his

*The first passenger-carrying train – the Directors' Special, 26 September 1877*

report before he wrote it. To test for vertical weight he used ballast engines, first one travelling across the girders alone, then two coupled together, then three, four, five, and finally six. He ran them at various speeds, the fastest at forty miles an hour, and on one occasion he climbed inside an iron pier of the High Girders, with his notebook in hand and his hat clamped firmly upon his head. Then he had it all done again while he stood on the south shore with a theodolite, directing it at the top of the High Girders to observe lateral oscillation. This, he later told the Inquiry, was 'nothing at all excessive, as my judgement went'. In all his tests he paid no great, if any, attention to the possible effect of wind pressure, and when he was asked why (since it was clear that this might have been a contributory cause of the disaster) he said 'The subject never entered into the calculations that I made, and never has done. It has never been, to my knowledge, customary hitherto to take wind pressure into account in calculating parts of bridges of this description.' The thought had occurred to him, however, and in his report – which passed the bridge subject to some trivial changes – he said that he hoped, should he visit the bridge again, to have an opportunity of observing the effects of a high wind when a train was crossing. Before he could make such a visit, those effects had been dramatically demonstrated.

The inauguration of a passenger service across the Firth of Tay took place on 31 May 1878, once more by the *Lochee* and carriages full of invited passengers. The general public had to wait until the following day, when they came early and in crowds to Tay Bridge Station, anxious to board the 6.25 a.m. and thereafter boast that they had been among the first to travel on the bridge. Apart from some indignation that the advertised price of the ticken had been raised from sixpence to ninepence, there was nothing but praise for a miracle of engineering which, as one said, could transport them through the air 'with the sea-mews wheeling beneath us'.

In the months that followed the North British was delighted to discover that the bridge had brought a prosperity beyond hope. The company was now carrying 84 per cent of the Dundee to Edinburgh traffic, and 59 per cent of that between Edinburgh and Aberdeen. Traffic between Dundee and Fife was doubled, season tickets had increased by one hundred per cent. The Fife coal-fields had been opened up to a degree impossible when the ferry-system alone had been in operation. Before the end of 1878, goods and mineral traffic into Dundee rose by 40 per cent, and there was no longer any doubt that the North British could and would dominate the railway industry in the north of Scotland. It had over 500 locomotives, one thousand carriages and nearly 30,000 wagons. It was carrying 15,000,000 passengers and taking a total revenue of more than £2,000,000 a year. One thing only was needed to make directors and shareholders completely happy, and that happened in June 1878. The Queen was persuaded to return to England from Balmoral by way of Dundee. She came one afternoon in the Royal Train, drawn by the engine *Netherby*. It is true she did not alight, did not step upon the great red carpet, but there she was behind a lowered window, an old lady in a poke bonnet, smiling gently. Bouch and others were briefly presented to her. She uttered a few words of sorrow about the tragic death of the Prince Imperial in Zululand, and then she waved and was gone. The *Netherby* travelled slowly over the bridge, and as it entered the High Girders the guns of the training-ship *Mars* fired a cotton-wool salute.

By the autumn of 1879 the novelty was fading, and the nation's imagination was now excited by another miracle to come. 'Except in matter of length,' said the press, 'the Tay Bridge will be a mere trifle compared with the Forth Bridge.' If familiarity had not bred contempt, it had brought criticism, some of it more alarming than was realised at the time. General Hutchinson had recommended a maximum speed of 25 miles an hour on the bridge, but many travellers were certain that this was being dangerously exceeded. Reputable gentlemen sat in their first-class compartments with watch in hand, or timed the trains from the ferry-boats and the shore. They concluded, and later declared at the Inquiry, that speeds of 30, 35, and sometimes 42 miles were being reached, and this by drivers who, as was well known, were racing the ferries. The Provost of Dundee suffered such 'mental discomfort' on the bridge that he gave up rail travel and returned to the boats. He complained about the speeds to the station-master and to Henry Noble, the resident inspector of the bridge. Noble did nothing, and the station-master little more than advise the drivers to 'go cannily' because the Provost was complaining. One driver said that he smiled to himself at this, 'thinking the whole thing perfect nonsense'. The Provost was not the only passenger to be alarmed by the curious movement of the bridge when a train was crossing. Others, many ladies among them, were frightened by what seemed to be a shaking of the girders, by the 'prancing motion' of the trains. A minister said that when passing through the central spans in a strong wind he was conscious of an extraordinary assault upon his ears. It was 'something similar to shocks of electricity, first in one ear and then in the other, something in the nature of a percussive effect'.

Painters who worked on the girders reported an alarming number of fallen bolts along the permanent way, and that on the lower piers they were rusting through at a startling rate. The vibration set up by trains passing above or below them as they worked, 'a good dirl' said one of them, also made them uneasy. He remembered that during a particularly fierce gale the force of the wind was too strong for him to work, and he was afraid to go out again. He had seen rents in the iron of the piers that supported the High Girders, but these had meant nothing to him, beyond the fact that he could sink the whole blade of a pen-knife in one of them. Noble had also found some of these faults, and ties loose in the cross-bracings. He did not tell Bouch, but packed the gibs and cotters with iron paid for from his own pocket. Bouch was informed that there were vertical cracks in several of the columns, and these were braced with wrought-iron hoops. Ill-health kept the designer from visiting the bridge as often as he may have wished, but he had every confidence in Henry Noble.

On Sundays the mail train from Dundee to Burntisland left Tay Bridge Station at 1.30 p.m., and began its return journey at 5.20, reaching Dundee shortly before 7.30. On Sunday, 28 December 1879, the Drummond tank engine which normally pulled this train was under repair, and had been replaced by an olive-green Wheatley bogie, Number 224. There were three third-class carriages, one second-class, one first-class, and a small brake van containing 46 bags of mail and other luggage. The length of the train was almost 225 feet, and its weight was 114 tons 14 cwts. Shortly after seven o'clock when it left St Fort, the last station before the bridge, it was carrying seventy-five passengers, and the storm which had been blowing along the firth since dusk was now extraordinarily strong.

It was an age of amateur meteorologists, and on Tayside that evening many gentlemen had been recording the force and nature of this unusual gale. More professionally, at Scotscraig a retired admiral registered a small eclipse of the moon shortly before sunset at 3.37 p.m. and was then driven into his house by a heavy fall of rain. As the wind rose, bracing up to heavy weather, he worried about an aged walnut-tree in his garden, and, more compassionately, expressed concern for all men at sea on such a night. He saw that there had been a sharp fall of the glass, so remarkable that he asked his servants if the instrument had been touched. At five o'clock the wind changed to westward, and he estimated it as between 75 and 78 miles an hour. Aboard the *Mars*, her captain had also noticed an alarming drop of the glass, and he logged the wind as Force 10 or 11, almost the maximum. He remembered a gale, little worse than this, that had mauled his ship at the mouth of the Plate, and he sent word along to make everything snug and fast.

By 5.30 the wind was punishing Dundee. There was a continual clatter of falling tiles and chimneys. A member of the congregation at Ward's Chapel later described the noise as 'a roll of iron plates'. A photographic booth at the top of Commercial Street exploded like a bomb, and a large wooden board, thirty feet in length, was blown from the top of Lamb's Hotel. Along the shore, below the new esplanade, the roofs of bathing-huts were ripped away, and heavy stones were drawn from the walls of a house in Wolseley Street. Called to the marshalling-yards, the station-master discovered that three laden coal-wagons had been blown four hundred yards up an ascending gradient. Passengers on the last train over the bridge, before the expected arrival of the 5.20 from Burntisland, were frightened by the violence of the crossing, and the guard said that £500 would not persuade him to go back that night. 'My coach was lifted from the rails and streaks of fire came from it.'

At seven o'clock the captain of the *Mars* logged a barometer reading of 29.00. Five minutes later a small turret was blown from St Peter's Church. At Scotscraig and looking from his window when there were fitful moments of moonlight, the admiral saw that his lawn was covered with broken branches, 'as if they had been wounded by round-shot'. The force of the gale, he decided, must now be 78, very bad for a country so far removed from the aerial violence of the China Seas. At twenty minutes past seven his gardener reported that the walnut tree was down, 'all gone smash'. This was the exact moment, as near as anybody could tell, that the High Girders plunged into the Tay, taking the 5.20 with them.

The disaster was witnessed – albeit unclearly – by many people who lived within sight of the bridge, and whose custom it was to darken their rooms, gather at the windows and watch the faery lights of a crossing train. The gale this night made the experience the more exciting. None could remember exactly what was seen, and there was conflict in small details when they appeared before the Inquiry, but they spoke of signal lamps boldly advancing and then disappearing, of flashes of fire, of great sparks, and then 'a mass of fire, gently falling'. One man only was more exact, an employee of the Caledonian Railway who lived on the Blackness Road. He left his house to shutter a window just before seven, and when this was done he walked across the road to look at the bridge and the arrival of the train. He was the only man that night that clearly saw what happened or who said he saw what happened.

As near as I could guess in my mind it would have been about the first girder or the second. I just immediately got nervous at once, and I rubbed my eyes. In a second or two I saw another lump going and just at that moment I saw the southernmost part of the high girder, I saw a blink of light and the blink of light had cleared away. The moon was shining as clear as could be on the river, and I saw the large piers from end to end.

He had not seen the train on the bridge, but believed it to be there. He saw no flashes of fire, no lights falling into the river, just that blink in the High Girders, and then the awful gap.

Along the north shore by Magdalen Green there was great alarm as men and women ran from their houses shouting that the bridge was down. It was still hard to believe, although there was no reply when a signal was rung to the cabin on the south. The station-master stood with his silent staff, all shielding their faces from flying splinters of glass, and wondering what to do. Then a locomotive foreman walked down the permanent way with the station-master, and out upon the bridge. They walked, and then crawled against the wind until the master was too giddy to go further. The foreman went on alone, upon his belly, and reached the great gap, lying there with a broken pipe spewing water above his head. When he returned, he reported that all thirteen of the High Girders were down. Since the 5.20 had been signalled on to the bridge, and since he could not see it on the line beyond the gap, it was undoubtedly gone with the girders.

*The high girders after the disaster*

Before midnight, and from then on until dawn, there were boats out on the restless river, their crews and their passengers calling to the darkness in the desperate hope that some survivors might be clinging to the broken piers. Great crowds filled the streets about the station, and the shores on both sides of the firth. There was a police cordon about the harbour, to restrain those who wished to hire boats and search for kinfolk they believed to have been on the train. Few people went to bed. Their windows remained lit, and those who could stared at the river beyond, as if they expected some miracle by which the bridge would re-erect itself and the train would steam safely into Dundee. The telegraph was busy, messages to John Stirling, to Thomas Bouch, to southern newspapers. They went by the Caledonian wire . . . *appalling catastrophe . . . terrific hurricane . . . Tay Bridge down . . . passenger train hurled into river . . . supposed loss of 200 lives.* . . . Before breakfast on Monday the weeping or silent crowds still abroad stared out across the now placid river, to the awful stumps, to the diving-boats clustered about them. There was no hope of survivors. 'The Queen is inexpressibly shocked,' her private secretary wired the Provost, 'and feels most deeply for those who have lost friends and relatives in this terrible accident.' Before shaving or eating, the Provost made the message public, and informed the secretary that nearly three hundred were believed to have been aboard the train.

The true figure, when corrected to seventy-five by the tickets brought across from St Fort, made little difference to the shock felt by the nation. Six hundred British soldiers of the 24th Foot had been killed in the Zulu victory at Isandhlwana eleven months before, but that valiant defeat had inspired pride as well as grief. In this calamity the greatest casualty was perhaps pride itself, the conceit that moves from boasting of its achievements to dismissing them as mere trifles compared with what it will yet accomplish. An explanation was required, less from Providence than from those who had proposed the bridge, designed the bridge, built and maintained the bridge. On Saturday, 3 January, while divers were still groping in the muddy darkness of the sunken girders, three members of a Board of Trade Inquiry began their hearing in the Assize Court, Dundee. They were the Wreck Commissioner, Henry Cadogan Rothery, a man of sharp independence of mind, Colonel William Yolland the Chief Inspector of Railways, and William Henry Barlow the President of the Institute of Civil Engineers.

The purpose of the Inquiry, at this stage and as Rothery explained, was to establish those facts which could be ascertained locally, and to that end the Court listened to evidence from the signalmen at the south end of the bridge, to ticket-collectors, station-masters, travellers, the captain of the *Mars* and the old admiral from Scotscraig, to residents of Dundee who had seen the disappearing lights of the train, and the Caledonian man who had watched the plunge of the High Girders. The most chilling evidence was that given

*The search for survivors*

by the divers, brought from their work to tell of their dark descent into the river, the tangle of girders they found there, wrecked carriages through which they had crawled and found no bodies. It was on Monday, the second day of the Inquiry, and at a moment when a witness was telling the Court how he had seen 'a mass of fire fall from the bridge', that the first body was recovered, drawn from the mud by a grappling-iron. It was identified as an employee of the North British, a guard, and the silver watch in his pocket had stopped at 7.16. His corpse was taken to a refreshment-room at Tay Bridge Station and there placed upon a wagon-sheet with its face uncovered. During the days following, this bright room of polished wood and bevelled glass would become a bizarre mortuary where relatives might recognise their dead, or the pitiful articles of clothing that could put a name to those yet to be recovered.

The Court sat for one more day, when Rothery declared that having exhausted all local witnesses the Inquiry should now adjourn until further evidence, relating to matters beyond the nature of the storm and the events of Sunday night, was available. When it re-assembled on 26 February, again at Dundee, thirty-three bodies had been taken from the river. More would be found, but twenty-nine were never to be recovered and perhaps still lie in the mud and clay of the Firth of Tay. The search for the dead was exhaustive, compassionate, and occasionally profitable, for the North British offered £2 for every body found (and was sternly criticised for lowering the rate from an original £5). A Relief Fund was established, to which the North British gave £1,000, Thomas Bouch sent a cheque for £250, and when the figure had reached £3,000 the ladies of Dundee organised genteel musicales to increase it. The last claim upon this fund would be made in 1938, by the aged sister of a guard who had travelled to his duty on the 5.20 from Burntisland.

The second hearing of the Inquiry lasted until 3 March, and now startling information about the construction, maintenance and operation of the bridge began to emerge. Upon the matter of the speed of trains, the drivers who were examined stubbornly claimed that they had never exceeded 25 miles an hour. Evidence given by passengers, however, contradicted this, and although the drivers further denied that they had raced the ferries across the river, it became clear that many people believed this was a common practice. If train and ferry left Newport for Dundee at the same time ('Chock and block, every morning full'), then the train would arrive in ten minutes and before the boat. If it were late in leaving Newport, however, it had to put on speed to match or beat the ferry. Drivers who stoutly denied that they had ever raced the boats, and who said that if they took six minutes to cross the bridge they could not reach Dundee in ten minutes, paradoxically admitted that they sometimes made the journey within that advertised time. Passengers who were not alarmed by excessive speeds seem to have enjoyed the boyish contests, but a railway clerk declared that when the hurrying trains took the curve into the High Girders he felt 'a sudden shock driving the carriage over, and then it gained its perpendicular'.

If the matter of speed was not satisfactorily determined, there was to be little doubt that work at the Wormit foundry had been appallingly, dangerously shoddy. The Court listened with chilled astonishment to the evidence of its workmen, to an explanation of that incredible substance Beaumont Egg. Dressers in the foundry said they had often seen holes in the iron cast, blow-holes which should have made its rejection obligatory. The holes might be only half an inch in diameter on the surface, but could expand two inches or more inside. One witness said that he had seen iron columns go on to the lathe 'quite whole apparently, and honeycombed after they were taken out'. They were not always discarded, 'but the honeycombed holes were generally filled up with Beaumont Egg, and the columns laid down with others to go to the bridge'. *What*, he was asked, *was Beaumont Egg*?

It is composed of bees-wax, fiddler's rosin, and the finest iron borings melted up, and a little lamp black. . . . You take a red-hot bar and melt it in, and it sets again like metal. It would not melt in the sun, but a man could pick it out with the point of a knife if he wished. If the column got a sudden shake, it would fall out.

Where was this remarkable substance acquired? From Fergus Ferguson, the foreman of the foundry. Another dresser admitted that he made the Egg himself, from materials bought with money given him by Ferguson. A third who told a similar story, admitted that the foreman had discharged him for drunkeness, and agreed further that he had been 'drinking somewhat' before his appearance this day. One happy drunkard, however, could not diminish the weight of this damning evidence.

Ferguson had already appeared before these dressers were examined. Still young, he was an arrogant and truculent man with obvious contempt for white-handed gentlemen who knew nothing of his trade and who now questioned his skill and integrity. He denied that he had ever used any substance to plug the blow-holes, although of course he knew of its existence. He admitted, without being aware of the gravity of what he was saying, that he had cast much of the iron according to his own reckoning of what was proper. He agreed that there had been a great waste of iron at the foundry due to unsatisfactory casting, although he managed to say this in a manner that demonstrated how conscientious he was. Under persistent questioning, he allowed that his original figure of 'thirty to forty at a rough estimate' for the number of columns he had broken up as useless, might in fact be nearer to sixty or seventy. Still examined on this point, he finally said 'I have broken up, I suppose, for one defect or another, about two hundred.' How many were not broken up but were sent out to the bridge, plugged with bees-wax, rosin and lamp-black, could only be guessed at. One counsel pressed the foreman hard to say which would be stronger, a lug moulded on a column or one burned on, asking the question three times without receiving an unequivocal answer. When it was put for the fourth and last time, Fergus Ferguson dismissed it with sullen contempt. 'I have answered the question perfectly well, and I will answer it no more.'

Gerrit Camphuis came before the Inquiry with confidence, the first important member of the contracting firm to appear, and one who had shared the responsibility for the foundry and the erection of the girders. His early self-assurance was quickly destroyed by an examination of his qualifications. His previous experience was largely administrative, and he knew no more of erecting girders than had been required by the building of a floor in one of his employer's workshops. 'I would not call myself an experienced founder and moulder,' he also admitted, 'but I can judge very well of foundry work.' Upon that claim he was asked to examine and measure fragments of iron which came from piers he had erected and which had fallen on the night of the disaster. He was forced to agree that there were improper inequalities in the thickness. Told that three pieces of the metal came from Pier 34, which he had inspected, he said 'If it was cast in my time, I do not think I should have passed it.' He was asked to examine a blowhole on the surface of the iron, and lamely agreed that there were small globules of cement in it. 'I should think it had been put in to fill up the hole . . . to hide it.'

The full story had not been told when the Inquiry concluded its hearing in Dundee on 3 March. When it assembled again, in London and on 19 April, there were more counsel present, now representing the interests of the contractors and of Sir Thomas Bouch. During the sixteen days that followed there was a painstaking examination of the design, construction and maintenance of the bridge. The first witness called was perhaps the most tragic of the whole Inquiry with the exception of Bouch – Henry Abel Noble, onetime assistant to the designer and later the resident inspector of the bridge during its brief life. His integrity was never in question, only his wretchedly inadequate qualifications. His strongest motive had been an admirable (in the context of his time, at least) desire to save his employers money, and he once undertook some river-diving himself, rather than ask the company to find the wages of a professional diver. The first question put to him was pitiless in the answer it wished to put on record. What had he been bred to? 'I was apprenticed to a bricklayer, and I am now an inspector of brickwork.' He had no engineering skill, and during his career as inspector of the bridge he had no assistance or guidance from anyone with such knowledge.

Q. No one was there to look after the ironwork of the bridge so far as it stood between the top of the pier and the bottom of the platform?
A. Except myself.
Q. You had no instructions?
A. I had no instructions?
Q. You did what you liked, if you thought it necessary for the purpose of the company?
A. Just so.
Q. Did no one inspect the bridge from the time you went there, which was in May, 1878, till its fall in December, 1879?
A. No one but me.

He had found faults, of course. There were cracks in the columns below the High Girders, some between four and six feet long. He took a page from his note-book, damped it with spittle, and pasted it across the crack. He waited until a train passed overhead, and since the paper did not break he decided that the crack was not widening. He then thrust a thin wire (from the stopper of a ginger-beer bottle) into the crack, and was relieved to discover that it did not go as far as the concrete core. He believed the bridge to be safe, but to make sure he bound this and other cracked columns with hoops of iron. He reported them to Bouch who, on a rare visit to the bridge, examined the first-aid and said he was satisfied. Noble had also discovered that the tide had scoured the river-bed at the base of some piers, and he ordered these holes to be filled with rubble. He found many gibs and cotters loose on the girders, and told no one, buying iron scraps from his own pocket to pack the loose metal.

Albert Grothe was summoned from Spain where he was then in employment. He told the Inquiry that in his opinion the bridge had been blown down by the wind, he could think of no other explanation. Could he say, as a civil engineer, what was the usual allowance for wind pressure? 'Upon this point,' he admitted, 'my notions have been very erroneous up to this time. They have been considerably modified by what I have heard since the Tay Bridge fell.' Disarming honesty was the tone of his evidence, even to admitting that there could have been botching and poor workmanship at the foundry, but in a large enterprise, employing six to seven hundred men, it was impossible 'to keep so strict an eye on everything'. He had never seen Beaumont Egg, not to know it as such. There had been an occasion, an inspection visit with his employer, when he had seen a small hole in the iron, filled with a foreign substance. 'The foreman was called, and got a severe scolding for not having prevented this.' Grothe admitted that he was not himself a practical iron man, not a man of much experience in foundry work. Neither was Mr Camphuis, who had administrative rather than technical charge. Who then, *did* have such charge and responsibility? The scolded foreman, Fergus Ferguson.

Thomas Bouch was called at eleven o'clock on Friday, 30 April, and despite the strain of the past months, the increasing risk to his reputation and his self-respect, he conducted himself with courage, and once with a touch of forgivable pride. When asked how many bridges he had designed, he declared 'I do not suppose anybody has built more.' He loyally defended the assistants who had helped him with his calculations, Noble among them, and he would not allow counsel to shake his faith in the type of bridge he had chosen to build. It was to a design 'which I had found from twenty years experience to be the best'. There had been nothing wrong with it. It fell, but not because of faults in design. During the days he had spent in Dundee immediately after the disaster he had formed his own opinion as to the cause.

Well, I have thought about it very anxiously, and my opinion is fixed now; that it was caused by the capsizing of one of the last, or two of the last carriages – that is to say, the second-class carriage and the van; that they canted over against the girder. . . . Practically the first blow would be the momentum of the whole train until the couplings broke. If you take the body of the train going at that rate it would destroy anything.

Cross-examination could not move him from this opinion, although he floundered in some of his replies to other, highly-technical questions. So much so that counsel tartly demanded 'Will you keep to one thing, if you please?' Bouch's reply was almost a plea for tolerant understanding. '*I am explaining* . . .!' Thereafter, when questions became pressing, he fell back again and again upon the honest if unsatisfactory reply 'I really cannot answer that, for my memory does not serve me.' Upon one matter, however, his answers were more direct, and probably ended any hope he may have had of emerging from the Inquiry without blame.

Q. Sir Thomas, did you, in designing this bridge, make any allowance at all for wind pressure?
A. Not specially.
Q. You made *no* allowance?
A. Not specially.
Q. Was there not a particular pressure had in view by you at the time you made the design?
A. I had the report of the Forth Bridge.

The Court knew from previous evidence, however, that the Tay Bridge had been under construction for nearly three years when Bouch received this report from the Astronomer Royal, with its vague generalisation about a pressure of 10 lbs to the square foot. It also knew, from evidence given by the Secretary to the Meteorological Council, that there could be heavy wind pressure indeed on the Tay, along a front of perhaps 250 feet, and that this pressure could be more than 50 lbs to the square foot. Finally, it had been told that the velocity of the wind along the firth could reach 90 miles an hour. These were the facts for which Thomas Bouch had made no special allowance.

The last body had long since been recovered from the Tay when the Court of Inquiry presented its reports to both Houses of Parliament in July 1880. Rothery thought himself obliged to submit his observations and conclusions separately. All three men were agreed in principle, but Yolland and Barlow were reluctant to make harsh condemnations. Not so Henry Rothery. 'It seemed to me,' he wrote, 'that we ought not to shrink from the duty, however painful it might be, of saying with whom the responsibility for this casualty rests.' And in saying so, he showed none of the compassion he had extended to Bouch during the hearing.

This bridge was badly designed, badly constructed, and badly maintained, and its downfall was due to inherent defects in the structure, which must sooner or later have brought it down. For these defects both in the design, the construction, and the maintenance, Sir Thomas Bouch is, in our opinion, mainly to blame. For the faults of design he is entirely responsible, For those of construction he is principally to blame in not having exercised that supervision over the work, which would have enabled him to detect and apply a remedy to them. And for the faults of maintenance he is also principally, if not entirely, to blame in having neglected to maintain such an inspection over the structure, as its character imperatively demanded.

The contractors and the North British were also condemned, but the great light of guilt fell upon Bouch, and it was the end of his career. His hopes, encouraged by some of his colleagues during the Inquiry, that he would be allowed to design a new bridge, were now destroyed. His associates withdrew their support and he was told that his services were no longer required. Four months later he was dead, the last casualty of his Noble Undertaking. In one sense he had been true to the Victorian ideal of self-help and success. This modest sea-captain's son died a rich man, leaving a fortune of more than £200,000.

If there could be no doubt now why the bridge had fallen, the exact manner of its collapse had been beyond the cautious conjectures of Yolland and Barlow. But not Mr Rothery.

What probably occurred was this. The bridge had probably been strained, partly by previous gales, partly by the great speed at which trains going north were permitted to run through the high girders. The result would be that, owing to the defects to which we have called attention, the wind ties would be loosened; so that when the gale of the 28th of December came on, a racking motion would be set up . . .

. . . with a strain upon ties and columns, lugs and bolts until the burden became intolerable. The bridge broke and fell, span by span, carrying with it an engine, five carriages, a brake van and seventy-five men, women and children.

# BIBLIOGRAPHY

## Thomas Muir

COCKBURN, H. *An examination of the trials for sedition . . . in Scotland* Kelley, USA, n.i. of 1888 edn. 1970.

COCKBURN, H. *Memorials* Mercat Press, n.i. of 1836 edn. 1971.

EARNSHAW, J. *Thomas Muir: Scottish martyr* Cremone, NSW: Stone Copying Co., 1959.

FERGUSON, W. *Scotland 1689 to the present* (Edinburgh history of Scotland, 4) Oliver and Boyd, 1968.

HOWELL, J. B. *State trials* Vol. XXIII.

INSH, G. P. *Thomas Muir of Huntershill* Golden Eagle Press, 1949.

MACKENZIE, P. *The life and trial of Thomas Muir, Esq.* Glasgow, 1831.

MEIKLE, H. W. *Scotland and the French Revolution* F. Cass, n.i. of 1912 edn. 1970.

SMOUT, T. C. *A history of the Scottish people, 1560–1830* Collins, 1969; Fontana, 1972.


## Patrick Sellar

ADAM, R. J. ed. *Papers on the Sutherland Estate Management 1802–1816* Scottish History Society, 1972.

GASKELL, P. *Morvern transformed* C.U.P., 1968.

GRIMBLE, I. *The trial of Patrick Sellar* Routledge and K. Paul, 1962.

MACKENZIE, A. *The history of the Highland clearances* A. and W. Mackenzie, 1883.

MACLEOD, D. *Gloomy memories of the highlands of Scotland* originally published as *History of destitution in Sutherlandshire* 1841.

PREBBLE, J. *The highland clearances* Secker and Warburg, 1963; Penguin Books, 1969.

RICHARDS, E. *The leviathan of wealth* Routledge and K. Paul, 1973.

SAGE, D. *Memorabilia domestica* Wick: W. Rae, 1889.

SELLAR, T. *The Sutherland evictions of 1814* Longman, 1883.

SMOUT, T. C. *A history of the Scottish people, 1560–1830* Collins, 1969; Fontana, 1972

## The Glasgow Cotton Spinners

ALISON, Sheriff *Practical working of trades unions* in *Blackwood's Edinburgh Magazine* vol. XLIII, March 1838.

BRASSAY, Z. G. *The cotton spinners in Glasgow and the west of Scotland c. 1790–1840: a study in early industrial relations* M.Lit. Thesis in the University of Strathclyde, 1974.

GLASGOW TRADES' COMMITTEE *The rights of labour defended* Glasgow, 1838.

MARSHALL, J. *The trial of the Glasgow cotton spinners for murder, conspiracies, committing and hiring to commit violence on persons and property etc.* Edinburgh, 1838.

MARWICK, W. H. *Short history of Labour in Scotland* Chambers, 1967.

SWINTON, A. *Report of the trial of Thomas Hunter, Peter Hacket, Richard McNeil, James Gibb and William McLean . . . for the crimes of illegal conspiracy and murder* Edinburgh, 1838.

TURNER, H. A. *Trade Union growth, structure and policy* Allen and Unwin, 1962. o.p.

## Madeleine Smith

ALTICK, R. D. *Victorian studies in scarlet* Dent, 1973.

BLYTH, H. *Madeleine Smith* Duckworth, 1975.

BUTLER, G. L. *Madeleine Smith* Duckworth, 1935.

HUNT, P. *The Madeleine Smith affair* Carroll and Nicholson, 1950. o.p.

JESSE, F. TENNYSON *Madeleine Smith* (Notable British trials) W. Hodge, 3rd edn. 1949.

LUSTGARTEN, E. *The woman in the case* Deutsch, 1955. o.p.

MORLAND, N. *That nice Miss Smith* Muller, 1957. o.p.

SMITH, A. D. *The trial of Madeleine Smith* Sweet and Maxwell, 1905.

## The Tay Bridge Disaster

ELLIS, C. HAMILTON *The North British Railway* Allen and Unwin, 1955. o.p.

PREBBLE, J. *The high girders* Secker and Warburg, n.e. 1975.

THOMAS, J. *The North British Railway* David and Charles, 1969.

THOMAS, J. *The Tay Bridge disaster* David and Charles, 1972.

# Index

*Acknowledgment is due to the following for permission to reproduce photographs:*

HENRY BLYTH Smith family page 95; FERGUS CAMERON James Cameron page 6; DUNDEE MUSEUMS AND ART GALLERIES completed bridge page 124 and fallen girders page 129; IAN GRIMBLE Patrick Sellar page 63; THE MANSELL COLLECTION Emile L'Angelier page 98, Blythswood Square page 102, court scene page 107, court exterior page 114; MITCHELL LIBRARY, Glasgow cotton spinners page 68, Black Boy Close page 71, Sheriff Alison page 79, Gallowgate page 85; NATIONAL GALLERIES OF SCOTLAND Thomas Muir page 14, Lord Braxfield page 26, John Inglis page 110 and front cover; COUNTESS OF SUTHERLAND Elizabeth Gordon Countess of Sutherland page 47; NATIONAL LIBRARY OF SCOTLAND Tolbooth page 32, Patrick Sellar page 39; NATIONAL MARITIME MUSEUM, LONDON convict hulk page 33; RADIO TIMES HULTON PICTURE LIBRARY mule spinning page 69; SCOTTISH RECORD OFFICE first train page 125; SCOTTISH TOURIST BOARD Dunrobin Castle page 54; TOM WEIR crofts page 56 and sheep page 59.